Acclaim for Marjorie McKinnon's books

"The information in the book is presented in a direct manner, which is very easy to comprehend. The writing does not consist of a lot of technical terms that are hard for the average person to understand. The book is written by a regular person, and intended for an average, regular person to read. This is one thing that makes McKinnon's book stand apart other books addressing this same topic."

—Kam Aures for *Rebecca's Reads*

"After finding Marjorie McKinnon and the support she offered, we are now into our program. Our first meeting was a huge success. Thank you Marjorie and God bless you for adapting this program for our survivors to follow. You have given survivors hope to continue on their healing journey."

—Donna Gustafson, Executive Director,
Sunrise Center Against Sexual Abuse

"I just want to tell you that you are an amazing woman and I want to thank you for sharing your story, life and truth in this book. I feel honored to know you, and like you, am dedicated to helping other women have and find their voice."

—Monteze Deputy, Victim Advocate

"...a magnificent book, written with such understanding of the pain a child goes through and the gates that are needed to get through and enter in order to heal. Such love and thought goes into this book of healing. I highly recommend it."

—Cheryl Newton-Boyer, Lamplighter Facilitator

"McKinnon's work, when used as an adjunct to therapy and/or support groups, offers 'hands-on' exercises which will facilitate and hasten the process of healing. I have personal experience with many of the tools the author presents and can attest to their usefulness."

—Marcelle B. Taylor, MFT

My fiancé has well over 200 psychological and self-help related books. Half way through *REPAIR Your Life* she simply said 'As it turns out—I only needed ONE book!' It's a hard journey of not feeling worthy of love. Of sabotaging your happiness and your relationships. We could fill this entire review of stories of struggles or how we almost destroyed ourselves, but I think it's most productive to say, if you want to heal and to have peace—get this book."

—*Two Healers*, Austin TX

IT'S YOUR CHOICE!
Decisions That Will Change Your Life

By Marjorie McKinnon

The Spiritual Dimensions Series

Loving Healing Press

Cover photo by Tom W. McKinnon, courtesy of Lauren Bumgarner.

Library of Congress Cataloging-in-Publication Data

McKinnon, Margie, 1942-
    It's your choice! : decisions that will change your life / by Marjorie McKinnon.
        p. cm. -- (From the spiritual dimensions series)
    Includes bibliographical references and index.
    ISBN-13: 978-1-61599-045-0 (hardcover : alk. paper)
    ISBN-10: 1-61599-045-3 (hardcover : alk. paper)
    ISBN-13: 978-1-61599-044-3 (pbk. : alk. paper)
    ISBN-10: 1-61599-044-5 (pbk. : alk. paper)
    1. Decision making. 2. Self-actualization (Psychology) 3. Success.
4. Change (Psychology) I. Title.
    BF448.M37 2011
    153.8'3--dc22
    2010020025

Distributed by Ingram, New Leaf Distributing, Bertram's Books (UK), Hachette Livre (France)

Published by
Loving Healing Press   www.LHPress.com
5145 Pontiac Trail   info@LHPress.com
Ann Arbor, MI 48105

Tollfree USA/CAN: 888-761-6268
London, England: 44-20-331-81304

Contents

To Lois, for her support and friendship

<table>
<tr><td>1</td><td># Purpose in Life</td></tr>
</table>

Henry David Thoreau, in *Walden*, wrote:

> "I know of no more encouraging fact than the unquestionable ability of man to elevate his life by a conscious endeavor... To affect the quality of the day, that is the highest of arts. Every man is tasked, to make his life, even in its details, worthy of the contemplation of his most elevated and critical hour."

Upon first reading these words, I felt their salve on my soul as I had pondered for decades, *why do humans exist*? This question has haunted man for centuries. Being born, living in "quiet desperation", and then dying, only to be forgotten, is not a sufficient reason. Why would God create so many individuals; yet only a few seem to impact mankind? Does that mean that the average person has no purpose; does not even need to be here? Is it all a cruel joke told by some masochistic creator of the universe? With such a belief system, we become only another grain of sand in an endless stretch of inconsequential beach.

To counteract the detrimental effects of such thoughts, we need to find a reason for individual existence. Over 400 years before the birth of Christ, Socrates said, "an unexamined life is not worth living". Centuries later, Peter, Paul, and Mary added, "The answer, my friend, is blowin' in the wind". In between, hundreds of poets and philosophers have created their own answers. Everyone has a theory and, like the blind men and the elephant, all are true. Yet, the intangible thread that runs through all of them cries for an individual purpose, one that is stitched together by the fabric of one's own life. For if there is any one truth, it is that we are all unique. From that uniqueness grows the potential to follow our own path—create our own purpose, our own reason to be.

One has only to look at faces in a crowd to see that we were all created different. That difference is not limited by facial characteristics. Behind each face is a different personality, a human with limitless possibilities. Sadly, most of them have no awareness that they can be whatever they want to be. Even if they have a vague sense that something beyond their current existence waits for them, they have no idea how to access the power to put it into play.

Some will climb to the greatest heights—world leaders, research scientists, and Nobel and Pulitzer Prize winners. Others will create a need, a cry in the wilderness. Hitler's reign ignited the genius of Churchill, Roosevelt, Eisenhower, and many others who joined together to bring peace to a world at the brink of annihilation and a deeper comprehension of what man's intolerance to man can bring. Thousands of potential purposes exist, a honeycomb of human activity buzzing with the sound of mankind.

To exist without a purpose is to drift rudderless in a sea that has no destination, under a sky that contains only blackness. To block out that reality, man creates numerous distractions. For if we are on any course at all, we are on a course towards death and with no purpose in our **life**, the reality of death becomes intolerable. But think what it could mean if each of us were to discover our own purpose, set it in motion, and realize its fullest potential. In making a contribution, not matter how small, we arrive at the niche our spirit craves. Behind the old philosophy, "a chain is only as strong as its weakest link," lies the truth of supposedly inconsequential contributions. All contributions have consequence, so a society is only as successful as its smallest contributor. If you see the complete picture of any meaningful event carried out by a significant member of society, you will see that no one succeeds alone.

Behind Charles Lindbergh's unprecedented non-stop flight from New York to Paris stood hundreds of others—his financial backers, the mechanics who serviced his airplane, *The Spirit of St. Louis*, the company who built it, the people who offered a tantalizing carrot of $25,000 to the first person to do it, and a mother who believed her son could accomplish anything. Lindbergh alone would never have flown his historic non-stop flight. So it is with any meaningful event or the success of any significant individual.

For every human who already is purposeful in their life, thousands are not. This is a sad commentary on the human race. Can we not decrease that number? In doing so, we can change not only the direction of mankind, but heighten the awareness of a world that still has many purposes needing to be filled.

Even if one did not ascribe to the highest achievement, there are—like pieces to a puzzle—many parts that make up a whole and an opportunity to be a part of that whole. Not all of us are queen bees. Some are worker bees and there is no shame and lack of glory in being such. I have had much of my greatest satisfaction in my "worker bee" activities.

What if we carried this a step further? What if, in addition to finding a meaningful purpose to life, we discover that death is not an ending, but rather a beginning? What if we truly came to understand that there is no such thing as death as we know it; that the reality of what happens when you stop breathing is that you simply step out of your body like one would shed a suit of clothes? That body is only a part of us. What if beyond the awareness of the body, there is an awareness of the soul?

The best way to start changing your life, so that you are more than just a grain of sand and so can grow to your fullest potential, is to develop healthy behavior patterns in six dimensions: mental, emotional, physical, spiritual, social and financial. Everything stems from one of these and only by all six working together at optimum level can you create your own perfect world. Before I begin examining how to make wise decisions in these areas, I want to spend a few chapters exploring concepts that will prepare you for the exciting journey you are about to embark on.

2   Quality of Life

Let us begin with the essential character of quality. Quality is a degree of excellence. We all have choices in which degree we would like to strive for. Are we content with the mediocre or, sadder yet, does even mediocre seem unattainable? Does just making it through a day indicate all we are capable of? If you believe this, you are not giving yourself enough credit.

At birth, we are all handed the promise of the highest quality of life. This can be defined as becoming all that we want to be, having all that we aspire to, and experiencing everything in the universe in which we have an interest. The lowest quality of life would then be the lack of these.

Our gifts at birth are endless: knowledge, visualization, foresight, prudence, awareness, sensibility, feelings, and so on. Yet, as we proceed through the early stages of life, most of us will lose these very promises. Sometimes we lose them through childhood traumas; sometimes through our own volition. As we do, we spiral downward, away from the highest quality of life that was our original promise. Distractions in life—some pleasurable, some not—keep us from missing what we no longer think we have. Periodically, we meet others who seem to have retained these gifts and are living orderly lives, fulfilling promises they made to themselves to achieve goals that give them a quality to their lives that we lack. We respond with envy, bitterness, and a belief that they must have luck that we don't. We become convinced at the unfairness of a universe that would give to one person success and to another failure, through what we believe to be no fault of their own. Having missed one of the primary stages of development in maturity—accepting responsibility for our own actions—it is easy to blame "them", the fortunate ones who have life handed to them on a silver platter, or so we believe.

It is often not until we reach our forties, and become tired of life not turning out the way we wanted it to, that we begin to honestly assess the role we played in our own failures. We want the quality of our life to improve. We want to fulfill that destiny we were convinced of when we were young. What happened? How did life go awry? We are forced to look inward, as Aristotle said, "an unexamined life is not worth living", the truism that we dismissed when we were younger as words that could only interfere with our trek in life.

As one man put it when asked what happed to the millions he had earned:" Some of it I gambled away, some I spent on women, booze and other pleasures, and the rest I wasted." The sad part of that story is that he continued to waste his life, died in agony, alone and bitter, with few friends, and estranged from all but one of his children. Sadder yet was the fact that he was one of the most intelligent and aware people I've ever known. He was also one of the most abusive. Perhaps this is why he wasted his life. Perhaps a part inside of him felt deep shame and "women, booze and other pleasures," were only distractions to keep him from thinking about who and what he really was.

It takes more than intelligence and awareness to discover the truth to life; it takes wisdom, the ability to gather from one's experiences the secrets to life. There is always a test to discover whether the quality of our life is at an optimum level. Sit quietly and listen to your inner voices. Are you happy? Do you feel satisfied with where you are in life? Do you look forward to each day with zest? Do you feel wonder, joy, and enchantment at your life on a daily basis? If the answer to these questions is no, then surely there must be information in the road you have taken that can lead you down a path of wisdom, altering your current existence for the better.

A gal I worked with a few years ago complained every time I returned from a deeply satisfying and adventurous vacation that it was unfair that I had terrific experiences while on vacation when hers were always so dreary. I had just returned from a trip to Oregon where I had visited friends, fished and hiked the Rogue River, and driven up to Crater Lake, one of the most scenic and spiritual places in the world. After listening to her sniveling, I told her she had the power to create her own terrific experiences. She questioned, "how"? I asked her what she had done on her last vacation. "Cleaned my garage," she snarled. I walked away shaking my head. It's not that my garage was never cleaned. I did it on weekends prior to the vacation as well as any other "dreaded" chores so that I could leave with a clean conscience and, more importantly, with a clean house. One can hardly complain about their problems if one has the ability to change them. Yet, we are all guilty of this. *Woe is me*, we say. *My life sucks.* Why has it turned out this way? It's almost comical.

The quality of life category can be improved on a continuing basis. Cooking, something I find deliciously satisfying (pardon the pun), becomes an adventure when I take a previously raved about recipe and try to improve it. I experiment, adding a dash of this, a bit of that; take out something else, etc. Then I taste it (also using my poor husband as a guinea pig). It either is an improvement and I feel satisfaction or it tastes horrible, in which case I start all over.

Even in my daily walk, I improved the quality of my life. When we lived in Colorado, I took a certain route every day. Knowing it would be a better cardiovascular exercise, I decide to jog for the first ten minutes. I only made it for three. That's okay; tomorrow I'll do five, the next day eight, until I reach ten. It's amazing how much better I felt when I returned home. One day, I decide to add a different road to my route. It took me past a lovely old red barn surrounded by horse corrals and a pond. My spirits soared as I walked around the property. At the end of the road, I saw a spectacular sunset framed by mountains and a lovely meadow with more horses, more ponds, and groves of trees. My old walk around the neighborhood was never the same. We have since moved to Arizona (more about that later) but I continue with my same thought patterns.

I don't necessarily try to improve everything I do on a daily basis. That would put too much pressure on me and I would lose sight of the tried and true stability points they put in my life. But sometimes it's necessary to go a little further, climb another mountain, and see what's on the other side of that meadow. Perhaps I will sing as I go, "Climb Every Mountain", "When You Walk Through a Storm", "I Believe", or any other courage and idealism songs I can think of. Or maybe I'm just in the mood to sing a silly song that gives me the giggles. It doesn't matter if I don't sound like Barbra Streisand. Who cares! I've just improved the quality of my life, lifted my spirits, and I like the sound of my own voice; so what does it matter?

Opportunities for improving the quality of your life lie in abundance on a daily basis. When I was working, I enjoyed laying my wardrobe out the night before. I checked colors, styles, which accessories would match, and so on. When I woke up in the morning, I was already in a good mood, knowing how well dressed I was going to look.

Years ago, I was at a wedding reception and found myself sitting next to a gal who, if she hadn't been so obese, might have been attractive. She was well-dressed and had a face that looked so expertly painted that I was almost in envy. I noticed that, despite the tantalizing food being passed around, she ate nothing. Upon striking up a conversation with her, I found out that she had gone to Merle Norman Cosmetics that morning and paid a great deal of money to have her face done.

"I'm wearing five shades of lipstick," she said, pursing her lips for my inspection. "I don't dare eat for fear of messing it up." She leaned closer to confide, "It cost me a lot of money. I had my nails done too," she added.

I looked down at her magnificently manicured nails. She had the loveliest hands I'd ever seen. I glanced at my own. The fingers were thin and bony; the flesh on my hands had enlarged veins and had aged before their time. I felt envy and was glad that this woman, who was almost 200 pounds overweight, would have at least one thing that she could take pride in, but saddened at the knowledge that this wonderful meal was being unappreciated because of an expensive make-over.

We all make choices on a daily basis regarding what we wear, what we eat, the type of entertainment we indulge in, the kind of people we surround ourselves with. Our perception of what's healthy is often out of whack. **Joy in life is free. All you have to pay is attention.** This means using our head as we weave through our day making choices. I like to use the scenario of two women who have different Mondays.

Let's call the first one Mary Jane. After having lain her clothes out for the next day, Mary Jane goes to bed early, gets a good night's sleep, awakes refreshed, goes for a 30 minute walk in the park across the street, comes home, does 20 minutes of transcendental meditation, eats a breakfast of whole wheat toast, a banana, a glass of orange juice, and a bowl of oatmeal. She packs a snack of celery and peanut butter and low-fat popcorn, and a tantalizing lunch to include a large chef's salad with tomatoes, lettuce, bell peppers, cucumbers, chilled asparagus, red onions, cubes of cheese, and slivers of ham and turkey, all with a delicious low-fat sesame seed dressing. She throws in a couple slices of garlic bread, lemon ice, and ginger snaps for dessert. She leisurely gets dressed, grabs her favorite bestseller to read at lunch, and is on her way. She arrives at work in a perky, good-humored mood, wishes her colleagues good morning, and plows through her day. During her lunch hour, she calls a friend and they decide to meet after work for dinner and a movie. Mary Jane has had a joyous day.

Our other female, Wilomena, starts her Monday in a different mode. She stayed up late the night before, drank too many glasses of wine with a friend, and, even though she's been telling herself she's going to quit, smoked a half a pack of cigarettes. She wakes up tired and crabby, and realizes that she didn't do laundry over the weekend because she had a lot of partying planned instead. She looks around at her messy home and cringes. She meant to clean the house but time just got away from her. She steps on the scale, sees that the 30 pounds extra weight she's carrying didn't disappear overnight. This makes her crabbier. She drinks four cups of coffee, with three spoonfuls of sugar in each, and decides to skip breakfast. That could help her lose weight. She throws on a wrinkled brown suit. She knows brown is not a good color for her but it's the cleanest outfit she can find. She sees a run in her nylons and this sends her spiraling into an even worse mood. She tears in to her drawer trying to find another pair and realizes that in addition to not cleaning house and not doing laundry, she also neglected to stop at Wal-Mart to pick up nylons. She hopes no one will notice, but realizes that it's going to make her self-conscious.

She arrives at the office in a foul mood and growls at her co-workers. She's tired from lack of sleep, slightly hung over from too many cigarettes and too much wine, and her stomach is growling. She rages inwardly at the unfairness of life that makes her work for a living when she could be home sleeping in. Her day gets worse. The copy machine is on the blink, her boss neglected to inform her that he was out today, and she has scheduled a meeting with his most important client who is in a worse mood than she is when he discovers the boss is absent. She stumbles through apologies, and then promises herself to look for another job. Her boss is a jerk anyway and even though she's worked there for eight years and has been promising herself to find a better job, this time she almost means it. Her lunch consists of candy bars, potato chips, and a soda from the office vending machine. By 5:00, she tells herself that all she wants is to go home and get caught up on chores, eat something healthy, and start her life over. The phone rings and it's Patty, her pal from the night before. Patty has a lot of problems and wonders if Wilomena would like to stop at Robbie's Bar for a couple of drinks. "What the hell," Wilomena says to herself; "a few glasses of wine would probably perk me up."

A while back, I was working a temporary secretarial position at Claremont Colleges. My boss, who was a wonderful woman and an extremely fair boss, had a behavior pattern that I found healthy. Once in a while, as she walked through the door, she would make an announcement: "I'm crabby today." I liked that. It meant that there was no need to take anything personal if she seemed out of sorts. Reporting your feelings to people is a great way to let others know not only where they stand, but also where you stand.

It's never too late to change your behavior patterns. Grandma Moses began painting in her seventies and lived to 101. She became the greatest folk painter that ever lived. One of her more famous quotes was: Life is what we make it, always has been, always will be." While this piece of wisdom has been stated many times and in many ways before, nevertheless, it is almost painfully true. I say painfully, because most people will hear these gems and disregard them. They sound nice but would take discipline to put into action.

Perhaps we are hampered in our search for something higher than mediocre by our low self-esteem. There is no shame in this. Almost everyone suffers from it at one time or another. What to do to overcome this? There are many guides in this area. Start with your childhood. Do you have unresolved conflicts? Are traumas hidden in that closet in your mind? Why not open the door and drag them out to look at? The truth can truly set you free. There is much help available to overcome childhood crosses; therapy, self-help programs, books and tapes on self-esteem building, exercises such as journal writing and talking into tapes about childhood pains, joining support groups, buying a copy of a program called *REPAIR Your Life* (if there is any sexual abuse in your childhood), and the like. There is no time like the present to clear your mind of negative childhood messages. Your parents may not have done the best job they could but that doesn't mean that you can't re-create your own happy childhood.

Once you work through this sometimes-enormous hurdle, you can begin practicing daily self-esteem. Here are a few rules to help you with this.

Remember that when someone approaches you in a negative or hurtful manner, they are making a statement about themselves, not about you.

If you look good, you'll feel better about yourself. This will increase your self-esteem enormously. If you need to lose weight, get started. If your grooming is less than perfect, work on it. Get a new hairdo; buy yourself some new clothes; get your nails done; go to that dermatologist about those skin problems that have always plagued you, or the orthodontist to get your teeth straightened. Whatever you don't like about your personal appearance, it can be fixed. Most of the glamorous stars in Hollywood don't look that way naturally. Without the right lighting, the right hairdo, or makeup, you'd never recognize them in a grocery store; and some are quite homely. Everyone is potentially beautiful. You need only find your own best assets and accent them.

Don't feed yourself negative messages. If someone pays you a compliment and you respond with "oh, I don't like my hair, it's too thick", or "I've always thought my eyes were too close together", your inner self believes whatever you tell it. Tell yourself every day that you are beautiful. Even negative messages like, "my co-workers don't like me" or "my husband thinks I'm too fat", when there may be absolutely no proof that any of these negative messages are true, can do nothing but work contrary to your own well being.

Reiterate those qualities you like about yourself whether it is your pleasant personality, your graciousness, your work ethnic, your sense of humor, or your intelligence. Make lists of those qualities and put them where you can read them every day.

Keep in mind that "owning your own stuff" brings positive self-esteem. If you are late to work and your boss reminds you of it, don't storm off angry with him or her and feeling like you have no worth. Accept the criticism and promise to do better. No one's perfect, least of all your boss. It's amazing how taking responsibility for your own behavior makes you feel more powerful.

Develop a hobby or interest that you have a flair for. Share your accomplishments in that area with others. You'd be surprised how good you'll feel once you see that you are unique.

Do something nice for someone else on a daily basis. You don't even have to point it out to them. The important thing is that you'll feel better about yourself once you do. You'll feel even better if it's your own secret.

Practice being gracious and non-judgmental. Most people can see the inner beauty in people faster than the outer beauty by their behavior. This oftentimes makes them appear beautiful. Remember the opening lines to *Gone With The Wind:* "Scarlet O'Hara was not beautiful, but men seldom realized it when caught by her charms."

Share what you are learning about yourself and how you are building self-esteem with others. When giving something away that has value, you earn more of it for yourself.

If you have judged yourself in the area of virtue—moral excellence—and find your life wanting, don't despair. An age-old philosophical question "Can virtue be taught?" Of course it can. If being dishonest is a behavior you have been cursed with, you can change it. It is your behavior. You own it. It may have been around for many years but so were horses and buggies. That didn't mean the automobile wouldn't appear on the horizon. It may take practice to set a new behavior in motion, but you can do it. I believe that most people are, as Anne Frank believed, "good at heart". You need only "want to change", take a long hard look at any quality in the area of virtue that is a part of your make up, assess honestly whether it is positive or negative and begin making adjustments. Take them in easy steps, one day at a time, and soon they will be a part of the new you. With your own shortcomings repaired, you'll feel better about yourself.

When you find yourself worrying about what other people's opinion is of you, keep in mind that most people are so self-absorbed that you need not worry about what they are thinking of you; they are too busy thinking of themselves.

Many people have discovered secrets to happiness and shared them with others in the hope that they would listen. Louisa May Alcott, one of America's most beloved authors, wrote:

> I do not ask for any crown,
> But that which all may win,
> Nor try to conquer any world,
> Except the one within,
> Be thou my guide, until I find,
> Led by a tender hand,
> The happy kingdom in myself,
> And dare to take command.

Oliver Wendell Holmes said: "What lies behind us and what lies before us are tiny matters compared to what lies within us." If only we could see that a joyous life is ours for the taking, we would not hesitate to locate the secrets and put them into use. This book contains most of them.

3 | The Interconnectedness of the Six Dimensions

Now, let us get to the meat of *It's Your Choice! Decisions That Will Change Your Life.*

There are six dimensions in life: mental, emotional, physical, spiritual, social, and financial. Webster calls these "one of the elements or factors making up a complete personality or entity. All else stems from one of these six. Nurturing all six is vital to one's total well-being. Making wise decisions in these areas on a regular basis promotes a more meaningful life. They are all integrated parts of a whole. One can expand one's mind, develop ideas and concepts in a pragmatic and orderly fashion, and yet be unable to love or be loved. That is not a whole person. One can be a Cardinal in the Roman Catholic Church, an idol in the eyes of one's parishioners, and yet be unable to communicate in an enjoyable, social environment. Again, that is not a whole person.

We all have skills in one area or the other. Few are skilled in all six. But that doesn't mean we can't strive to be competent in all of them. With a natural flair for communication, one individual can be a socially skilled human and perhaps even a mentally gifted one. That same person may even be naturally inclined to make wise financial decisions. But perhaps keeping in shape physically, watching their diet, and utilizing preventive medicine skills is not something they are adept at. One can easily see that without optimum physical health, the mental, social, and financial skills one day may be a moot point. All six need to function together in a healthy manner.

Like an orchestra that, without the grand piano, or with no violins or percussion, no brass or woodwinds, would not sound as harmonious, the physical body needs all instruments working well together. Our ego, that is, our inner self, knows how to pull the best performance out of each of our dimensions. All we need do is listen to our inner self, that internal voice that knows more than we realize.

The central and most important part to our being is the soul, the part of us that no one can prove to exist. And yet it does. It is the only part of us that is eternal. It is like the conductor that draws out beautiful sounds from his musicians. The soul has the power to kindle and awaken, to evoke the beautiful music that lies waiting in all of us. Never underestimate that soul part of us.

When I was a child, I read a book that held such fascination for me that I read it over a dozen times. It was called, *The World Would Be Well*. It was the history of medicine, told at the level of a twelve-year-old. Instinctively, although the book was about healing the body, I knew there were other dimensions that needed care as well. As I read through this history of medicine, I saw the development of mankind unfold in the arena of understanding the care and inner workings of the body as well as finding cures for disease. I followed the paths of learned and famous persons such as Louis Pasteur, Edward Jenner, Madam Curie, and Florence Nightingale, and thought about a "world that would be well." This book was monumental in the early development of my thirst for an understanding to the meaning of life. It planted seeds, not only in the area of wanting good physical health, but the question of what other parts to my being needed good health as well.

As I grew older, I was exposed to books that began my spiritual development. *The Lives of The Saints* and *The Catechism*, both staples for a devoutly religious Catholic family, were two examples. Once becoming an adult and out of the clutches of the church, I read The Baghavagita, The Koran, the teachings of Buddha, and various other works from world religions. They expanded that soul part to me more than I realized. I learned Transcendental Meditation and began practicing it on a daily basis. In my forties, I went back to college and took classes in Art, Archeology, World Religions, Political Science, English, Nutrition, and Philosophy. I learned about Aristotle, Plato, Socrates, Emmanuel Kant, St. Thomas Aquinas, Descartes, and a host of other philosophers. Even the teachings of Confucius profoundly affected my thinking. I studied Astrology for several years to assess the impact that the constellations and planets might have on our life. I soaked up like a sponge anything meta-physical, that division of philosophy that is concerned with the fundamental nature of reality and being. My thirst for knowledge grew.

Once I entered recovery, I was ripe to find out about the inner workings of the mind and the effect that childhood traumas have on your life. Working my way through five years of this was the best gift I could have given myself. I read many books on mental and emotional discipline, how to make wise decisions, how to overcome the ravages left by childhood sexual abuse. I listened to tapes, wrote letters to myself as well as to those who were deceased that had hurt me. I kept a daily journal on the progress of my recovery and both spoke in to and listened back to hours of tapes that I made, regarding my own "examination of conscience". I practiced a rigorous and healthy Twelve Step Program, one of the greatest tools available to mankind. And so my mental health improved as I laid the groundwork for future healthy decisions in that area.

I also began working in the Preventive Medicine Department of a leading Health Maintenance Organization (HMO). There I learned about cholesterol, diabetes, nutrition, smoking cessation, and exercise. I learned what part taking care of your body could play in taking care of your mind and your emotions. I learned how smoking just one cigarette could damage your body; how the primary practice in good nutrition was variety: vegetables were great, but not if you ate the same one over and over and nothing else.

We are fortunate to live in an age that understands good health is not limited to physical well-being alone. Today, there is a source for every dimension. We not only have doctors, nurses and dieticians for the physical part of us, we have accountants and financial advisors for the financial part, therapists and psychologists for the emotional side, ministers, rabbis, and priests for the spiritual side, teachers and philosophers for the mental side, and even experts in social skills can be hired to polish up that part of our life. As if that weren't sufficient to guide us in the right direction, there are numerous books, tapes, lectures, Twelve Step Programs for every problem, and other groups to add to the pile of resources. We need only avail ourselves of them.

This, of course, will get us nowhere without motivation. What is your motivation? We all have them. As an example, I've been asked why I look so young for my age. I always respond, 'vanity'. That may sound silly, but the truth is, I don't like not looking good. I've discovered that there are days when my emotional well-being is directly proportional to how good I look that day. That means not only dressing well, but also good skin care, good exercise, sleeping on my back, keeping my hands off my face (causes wrinkles), avoiding cigarettes and alcohol, the sun, and especially, bitterness.

Years ago when I read that sleeping on your stomach causes wrinkles, I was dismayed. I'd never slept any way other than on my stomach. There was no way I was going to train myself to sleep on my back or side. But the more I thought about it, the more sense it made. So one day I slept on my side. After a few nights, I felt comfortable with the change. Soon, I switched to sleeping on my back and today, I can't possibly sleep on my stomach. Vanity is often a misunderstood word. Webster says it is the fact of being vain or useless but it also says it denotes self-satisfaction. That can be a great carrot. How rewarding life would be if everything we did brought self-satisfaction!

All you need is to find your carrot. Many a wife, at the thought of losing her husband to another woman, was motivated to lose weight, learn how to cook, and keep a cleaner house. How many children, the closer to Christmas it gets, begin keeping their room cleaner and getting better grades? Discover your carrot. We all have one. Then get to work putting together a program to change your life.

4 | Perception vs. Reality

Before we begin integrating these six dimensions, we must learn about truth. Not the truth where we don't tell a lie, but the truth of seeing things as they are, not as we want them to be. It is said there are three realities: the way others see us, the way we see ourselves, and the way we really are. Are all three true, or is there one reality and the others but mere perceptions? The world, we found out as we grew older, is not black and white; it's made up of many gray areas. Emotions can particularly color our perceptions and blind us to reality. Often, once the event that has colored our perception has passed, it is easier to see the reality. By then, it may be too late.

A man who shoots his wife because he found her in the arms of another man, only to find out later that the other man was her long lost brother, cannot go back and undo his action. This is an exaggerated example of perception vs. reality. In real life, there are many day-to-day events that change our behavior to that which we later regret. How to see reality?

There are many ways of dealing with this. Objectivity is needed, as is reason. Emotions are not bad. It is what we do as a result of them that may not be the healthiest choice. Braiding our emotions with reason is not something most humans are adept at. When we are angry, we react. When we love, we are blind. When we mistrust, it is difficult to see whether there is any evidence to support our feelings. In truth, we are usually so overwhelmed with our emotions that even if someone had proof that they were incorrect, it would be difficult to pull away and see reason.

In order to develop healthy behavior patterns in any one of the six dimensions, it is imperative that we learn new skills in seeing reality as opposed to perception. It would never do for a man who was intending to save towards his retirement to frantically invest in a stock that appeals to him emotionally (stocks relating to an item, that is, becoming passé because his father worked in that field), only to find out that a little research would have told him he was going to lose money if he did so.

Someone reaching out for spirituality and finding themselves in the midst of a cult is going to have a long road back once reality sets in. Therein lies the crux of this matter. Reality usually does set in. Unfortunately, it is often long past the time when we can save ourselves from unfortunate consequences. How about the impulsive teenager who is caught in the throes of love and winds up having sexual relations with a man who she is convinced loves her deeply, only to find out after becoming pregnant that she is only one in a long line of sexual experiences that mean nothing to him? Her perception, that he loved her, and the reality, that he didn't, are going to be a painful lesson.

One of the primary ingredients necessary in identifying reality as opposed to perception is maturity. A relationship between two people who are both immature has little chance of succeeding. A relationship that has one immature person and one mature person has a better chance. But, obviously, the one where both have maturity has the greatest chance of success. This is the couple that will see reality in a situation and not be bogged down by perception. Sometimes, "wearing rose colored glasses" is another description of perception. We always want to believe that our positive perceptions are reality. That is called optimism. Optimism is good. Optimism without reason is not. A paranoid person, who sees the worst in everything as his perception, is usually delighted to see that his perception is also the reality.

But this is no way to run your life. So we come to the question: How does one achieve maturity? Not an easy task. What then is maturity? It is behavior and responses based on slow and careful consideration. Impulsive and rash decisions without benefit of reason will usually get you in trouble. This does not mean the absence of spontaneity and playfulness in your life. Spontaneity is natural, unrelated to any controlled or manipulated environment. Rash behavior is unthinking, a lack of consideration or caution. The woman who rushes out to spend $1500 for a new computer because of the advertising at her local computer store, then finds out the next day that the same computer was one-half less at a different store, is guilty of rash behavior. She will, no doubt, feel depression over this, unless, she has the moxie (mental dimension) to take it back, get her money returned, and buy the same computer at the other store. She has been able to turn her unhealthy choice around, but it has cost her time and frustration. Thinking this decision through would have saved her both.

And so it is with any choice throughout our day. The good news is that, while thinking things through is a part of maturity, once you put it in practice, it becomes automatic and that is when you have achieved true and functioning maturity.

One last word about maturity. It has been my observation that most people who I define as mature have their "wants vs. needs" clearly understood. We all have both but unless we take care of the needs, the wants are only superfluous and may even be harmful. For example, someone with serious heart problems may want to smoke (since he's done it for thirty-five years), but he may need to stop in order to stay alive. Someone else may want to overeat (since food is their drug of choice) but may need to diet and exercise. Wants are wonderful. We want to go on a vacation, but may need to save money towards it. We may want to call in sick because we need a mental health day. But if we've already used up our quota in that area, we may need to bite the bullet and go to work. The main difference in these two, wants and needs, is that maturity is required to differentiate between them. If you are taking care of all your needs (those things in life required to maintain a healthy environment), then go ahead and indulge yourself in all your wants.

5 Reducing Choices To Pragmatism

Fast on the heels of perception vs. reality is pragmatism, a philosophy developed by Charles Saunders Pierce. It assesses the meaning of what we say by its practical consequences. I've often referred to it as "that which works". In a perfect world, we would all live orderly lives, making wise decisions as we see down the road what the results of our actions are going to be. Some people are already blessed with this attribute. I know many people who schedule their tax appointment the first week of January, keep an orderly account of their finances so they can live within their means, plan their vacations months in advance, started their retirement fund at age twenty-five, bring a grocery list (and coupons) with them to the market, and so on. If they couple these skills with an appreciation of the arts and nature, the ability to be playful and spontaneous, a disciplined life and joyful environment, a spiritual base, as well as a host of well-adjusted friends and loved ones in their daily lives, then they are truly blessed.

But not all of us are like that. Henry David Thoreau observed in *Walden* that "the mass of men lead lives of quiet desperation." What a sad, but true testimony. I once asked a former doctor of mine, "How many of your patients are dysfunctional?" He replied, "They all are." What is the reason? We all have childhood traumas to varying degrees. Some work their way out and some don't. The ones that do will have a greater chance of not leading lives of quiet desperation. Even those who don't could begin to lead joyful lives if they threaded their choices with pragmatism.

This is not to say that we shouldn't listen to our own inner voices. We all have the truth within us. A warning bell sounds inside of us when something is not okay. Do we listen or do we ignore it? Listening to your own inner voices, your intuition, is a skill that can be fine tuned over the years and, like maturity, become an automatic reaction.

I believe so strongly in our own inner voices that I want to elaborate on them. Everything you experience through all of your senses goes somewhere into your unconscious. It may be only a fleeting fragrance, a short-lived glimpse, the light touch of another on your arm, gone from your mind the minute they've removed their hand, or the faint sound of a wounded bird. Each one is indelibly printed into your inner psyche. Picture a thousand creatures, infinitesimal in size, living inside of you. Each event in your life, no matter how minor, goes to them. They race around madly, storing it in a file somewhere that only they are aware of. They know that one day you will need to access that file and they are fully prepared to find it instantly and hand it to you.

Let me illustrate this further. One day, when you are five years old, you are taking a walk. It is a spectacular autumn day in southern Missouri. You pass a maple tree that is resplendent with beauty. The gold and russet colors mesmerize you. It is the largest maple tree you've ever seen, with winding roots trailing its base, twisting and turning like roadways in an ancient forest. A gray squirrel with a huge, almost flowering tail scampers up and down its trunk, his mouth filled with nuts as he looks for a home to deposit his find. You watch as you stand underneath the tree, feeling the slight breath of autumn stroking your cheek and thinking of the joy inside of you at the sight of this magnificent tree and the lively squirrel. For that moment, life is perfection.

An elderly lady approaches that has a birthmark on her face. You glance at her and keep walking. In a few seconds you hear horrible screeches, turn around, and see two of your classmates making fun of her. You are appalled, and the next day, chastise them at school. Many years pass. You have a faint memory of something from your childhood that captured your soul for a brief moment and would give anything if you could remember where it was and what was happening that you so treasured in your memory. It is all so foggy that at times, you wonder if you imagined it. You are now an elderly lady in your eighties. You are walking down the street and a rheumatoid, elderly man with a cane, hobbling on the sidewalk, slowly passes you. You hear the jeers of two young boys and glance behind you. All of a sudden, like a dream that came to life, everything you experienced at the age of five reappears in all its vividness. You see the cherished maple tree, you see the squirrel looking for its home, you feel the breath of autumn stroking your cheek, and the purple of the sky is even more vivid than you remembered. For one brief moment, you are flung back in time to re-experience a joyful memory when life was perfection.

It was all there, all the time. You needed only a trigger to recapture the memory. Life is like that. Everything is stored and nothing is wasted. Even incidents that you witness, that are lessons to be learned, lie in wait. Perhaps one day, you watched someone step in to a street without looking, only to be run over by a car. Your common sense will forever remember to look both ways. Lessons others have learned, if you pay attention to the witnessing or the hearing of them, are all lessons you too can learn.

I have a daughter who is in her mid-forties. When she was in her teens and had just bought her first car, she ran out of gas and called me to bail her out. I showed up with the obligatory can of gas as well as the statement that I would only do this once. I had every reason to believe that it would only take her once to learn. Not so; she still runs out of gas. She's bright, aware, sensitive, and has all the qualities one could have to make wise decisions. But she continues to have a more difficult life than she needs to. I told her one time that all of her problems could be resolved with two words. When she asked what they were, I replied, "Think ahead". She looked impatiently at me as if to say, "Jeeze mom, is that all?" She was unable to see that something so simple could be such help. Like all of us, she has all knowledge and wisdom inside of her and needs only to access it with pragmatism.

6 | Making Wise Decisions

As preparatory work for positive growth in the area of the six dimensions, a few words about making wise decisions are in order.

It seems like a simple statement. How do we even recognize what a wise decision is? When I was in recovery, my daughter (the same one who runs out of gas) gave me a book called *I Never Knew I Had A Choice*. All I needed to read was the title. I got it. Most adults that come from a dysfunctional family background don't realize that while, when they were younger, choices were made for them, not all healthy; as a grownup, they can make their own.

One of the things a counselor asked me to do, while I was in recovery, was to go home and eat dessert first. I thought that was a silly homework to prescribe. Of course, I can go home and eat dessert first. Not so. It took me several weeks to give myself permission to do it. A dozen unsaid, but still buried in my memory, instructions from my parents paraded back and forth: No dessert till you eat your dinner! A time and a place for everything; dessert is at the end of the meal! You'll ruin your appetite! And so on. Today, I often eat a lemon ice before I tackle a mushrooms-and-pasta dinner.

Not that eating dessert first is the epitome of wise decisions, but it's a good example of how we allow childhood messages to interfere with the unfolding of our own happy life. Everything we do throughout the day involves decisions: what time to get up, what clothes to wear, what to eat, how to speak, what kind of mood we're going to be in, how to spend our paycheck and so on. Sometimes, each decision involves more decisions till a labyrinth of choices faces us as the day goes by. Making the optimum one in each will ease our passage. And learning from the unhealthy ones we make, so that future decisions are better, is part of the decision-making process. No one makes wise decisions on a continuous basis. Not beating yourself up when you've made the wrong choice is also part of the learning process. Thinking things through helps.

One of the most amazing things I learned in recovery was that I did not have to make a decision immediately on anything. If someone asked me to join them after work, there was no harm in responding, "Can I let you know later?" Even someone asking a personal question, which I used to feel compelled to answer, even if I didn't want the asker to know the answer, became agonizing to decide. Should I be rude and say "none of your business"? Should I respond honestly, giving out information that I really didn't want to share? One way to deal with this is to ask a question in return. "Why do you ask?" It will buy you time. Answering a question with a question of your own often sets the tone for who has personal power in a situation. Better yet, a simple and gracious, "that's sort of private" can suffice. You are in charge of the words that come out of your mouth as well as the thoughts that enter your brain. And no one, I repeat, no one, can force you to do something you don't want to do. There may be repercussions that will be unpleasant if you don't comply, but that too is your decision. They may be worth it.

To me, just knowing that whatever happens in my day is a result of decisions I will make, makes me feel powerful. As long as I am prepared to accept the consequences of my own actions, I am free to do whatever I want. That kind of freedom is an awesome responsibility, not to be treated lightly. Since you only have so many hours in each day and so many days in each week, and so many years on this earth, why not strive to make all of your decisions as healthy as possible? If you don't start now, it may be too late. You don't want to wake up at 85 and start listing all your regrets.

7 | Master of My Fate, Captain of My Soul

It takes courage to change your life. Since life may come hard for some of us, let's take steps to "encourage" it. Part of what happens in courage is that it makes us the center of the spotlight, even if we're the only audience. In changing your life, you have to make a leap of faith. Fear often follows a decision to make a change. Where do we get the courage?

Courage comes in the day-to-day struggles that we all face. Courage comes in moving through tragedy, making unfamiliar choices, and heading in directions where there is an unknown result. But we've all done it. No one on planet earth has gotten where they are without courage. But it needs validating in order to see the reality of what a courageous being we really are.

Make a list of everything you've ever done that required courage. This will include anything that frightened or intimidated you. Leave nothing out. It may be something that seems trite, like learning to drive a car. Put it down. As you work through your list, you will discover something amazing—you have never given yourself credit for having courage.

When I first did this, I was almost embarrassed. My list included what I thought were silly things like diving off a high board at the age of eight when my knees were knocking, riding on the back of a motorcycle when I knew I was going to die, overcoming my fear of flying, raising four children by myself, climbing a cliff several hundred feet to its top despite my fear of heights, and so on.

Once you do this, you will begin to see yourself in a different light. There's something about knowing how brave you really are that causes you to forge ahead with your dreams. Courage is nothing more than a state of mind and you have the power to place yourself in that state of mind. Most people think of courage as something larger than life, a soldier in battle fighting for his country, a skydiver jumping from a plane, a blind man climbing Mt. Everest, and so on. Courage is more compelling when it is seen in the day-to-day challenges that people face, never knowing they could.

Let me give you another scenario that might change your mind about being courageous. If your doctor said you had six months to live and recommended that in the time you have left, you do everything you ever wanted to do, what would that list contain? Have you always wanted to sky dive, or climb cliffs, or maybe live alone in the woods for a month but were afraid you might be harmed? Maybe you've always had a fear of flying. What difference would it make if you now attempted it? You'd almost certainly live through it and it would enrich the time you had remaining. Wouldn't it be nice to go out saying you'd faced all your fears? Why wait till you have a death sentence? If it's that important to you, do it now.

William Earnest Henley penned some of the strongest words ever written about courage. When I first began this manuscript, I included them in this chapter. Then, before I had completed the book, Timothy McVeigh, the man behind the Oklahoma City bombing that killed hundreds of people in 1995, decided at his execution that the words to Henley's famous poem were the final ones he wanted to say before exiting his life. I found his actions disturbing in the extreme. It is a wonderful poem, meant to instill courage in people. Murdering hundreds of people did not take courage. It was an extreme act of cowardice. It's unfortunate that he was so unhealthy that he latched on to these wonderful words to illustrate his point.

I thought long and hard about whether to keep these words out of my manuscript. I didn't want them to be linked in any way to a mass murderer. But they had been, and hopefully, those of us who are enlightened realized that a very sick human chose inappropriate words to justify his actions. I decided that I was not going to allow that to cause me to delete these words. Since I seem to be quoting many famous words to illustrate a point, I think they bear adding to the list. They are from a poem called "Invictus" and were written after much soul searching by an individual who had merit and would no doubt be seething in his grave if he knew they were used for a purpose he never intended them to be. The last two lines are the ones most often quoted, but the entire poem bears hearing

> Out of the night that covers me,
> Black as the pit from pole to pole,
> I thank whatever gods may be
> For my unconquerable soul.
>
> In the fell clutch of circumstance
> I have not winced nor cried aloud.
> Under the bludgeonings of chance
> My head is bloody, but unbowed.
>
> Beyond this place of wrath and tears
> Looms but the Horror of the shade,
> And yet the menace of the years
> Finds and shall find me unafraid.
>
> It matters not how strait the gate,
> How charged with punishments the scroll,
> I am the master of my fate:
> I am the captain of my soul..

<table>
<tr><td>8</td><td># Preparing for Life,
Preparing for Death</td></tr>
</table>

Before we begin studying wise decisions in the area of the six dimensions, a word needs to be said about preparing for life and preparing for death. In order to tie the six dimensions together, one needs to see a global view of life, often referred to as "the big picture". Some of us are best at seeing the forest and others at seeing the trees. Blessed indeed is he who can see both, switching back and forth as if working on two different computer screens.

If we can look at the picture of "us", human beings, as on a long journey, one that begins with life and ends with what is often termed death, it will be easier to prepare for your own death. I prefer to call it "dropping your body" since I think the term death has, by definition, an incredibly negative and frightening connotation.

As babies and then children, we have little say in how to prepare for our own life. We may say to our parents as a young child that we'd love to be an astronomer or a doctor when we grow up, but how many of us have parents that say, "That's great Fred, we'll sign you up for medical college as soon as you turn twelve, and in the meantime, we'll buy as many medical books as we can to help you get started"? A few are blessed to have parents like that, but it's the exception, not the rule. Rather, most of us either don't take the steps to head in a certain direction as soon as we get out of high school, or maybe still have no idea what we want to be when we grow up. Often we just fall in to our "chosen" profession and at the age of 50 say, "I always wanted to be an astronomer". In a perfect world, all parents would pay attention to their children as they grow up and notice where their interests lie, then foster that dream as much as possible so that it can be a reality.

When my husband Tom was eight years old, he wanted to be a cartoonist. He had a natural talent for drawing as well as a marvelous and unique sense of humor. He took the initiative to write a letter to Walt Disney Productions to ask them how to make that happen. They sent him a Walt Disney postcard and a *20,000 Leagues Under the Sea* movie poster along with an encouraging letter, suggesting he attend art school and develop a portfolio. What a wonderful start for his dream. His parents told him that drawing was a waste of time and discouraged his dream. Years later, he had an Aunt Opal who was sixty when she began painting. Much was made in the family of her talent and why hadn't she started when she was younger.

These were bitter words for Tom to hear as he remembered his own, fallen by the wayside, childhood dream. When he became an adult, he fell into a job working as a lineman for Southwestern Bell; then went on to be a communications technician. While he mostly enjoyed his job, he never forgot the vision of an eight-year-old child. Over the years, he continued to dream of being a cartoonist even going so far as to purchase a drafting table and various brushes and pencils for the craft. He frequently doodled and drew cartoons that he shared with his co-workers; one in particular came back to him on the Internet twenty-five years later as being the focal point of a Drew Carey episode, with no credit, of course, to Tom.

His drafting table, which previously had gathered dust in our studio, came alive when he illustrated my book *REPAIR For Kids*. He is currently getting ready to illustrate *REPAIR For Toddlers*. Now that he's retired, he can finally pursue his childhood dream. Does this story sound familiar? Were dreams developing in your child's mind that never came to fruition? Is it really too late?

As I previously cited in the example of Grandma Moses, who didn't begin painting till her seventies, it's never too late to pursue your childhood dreams. Start preparing for your life. Are you happy doing what you're doing for a living? For that matter, are you happy with what you do in your spare time? If the answer is no and you're not sure what you'd like to be doing instead, begin making lists of where your interests lie. Then make lists of what you'd need to do to get there.

When I was very young, I knew I wanted to be a writer. My friends in Nebraska tell me that when I was in my teens, I was writing a novel (no idea what happened to it) and had already written dozens of poems. I read voraciously, always studying the various styles of writing, and thinking about what I could do with words. I was never encouraged in that area even though writing, spelling, and literature were subjects I excelled in. It wasn't until I turned forty that I actually sat down and wrote a serious novel, a mystery called *When First You Practice to Deceive*. Even then, I didn't think about selling it. I only knew that I had words inside of me that I wanted to put into prose or poetry. I have now written twelve books, four of which I've sold, and five volumes of poetry. I have three more that I am currently working on. I can't *not* write. The good news is that I will not have to die without having followed my natural bent.

Much like a tree with limbs that want to grow a certain way, humans too want to grow a certain way. To force that limb by binding it with wire to grow in a way other than it's intended is cruel. A person with creativity buried inside of them screaming to surface, but who works an unrewarding job as a supermarket clerk, is not going to enjoy his day. The yearning of a dream trapped within his body will be buried forever in a locked room in his mind.

Nothing is more important than freedom; freedom of thought, freedom to choose your own spiritual path, freedom to make all of your own choices and, especially, freedom of the spirit. The human spirit needs to soar, like a bird, to its highest potential, stretch its limbs to grow as far as they want, experience all the joy that sits and waits for them to take advantage of it. Start preparing your own life, no matter how old you are.

Now let's go to the other side of the coin, death. The study of philosophy has often been termed the study of the preparation for death. There is more truth to that than appears at first glance. We spend all of our life preparing to live it only to find out at the end that we didn't prepare well and now we must prepare for death. While these may sound like sad words, they don't need to be.

Preparing for death is another one of those realities that, until we begin to approach it, we see only as a perception. When we are younger, death is something that happens to sick and old people; but surely by the time our years have advanced, we will find a way to escape it. We don't actually tell ourselves this, but we live our lives as if it were true. But it is not. Death is the strongest reality there is.

How then does one prepare for it? Better yet, why should we? It'll happen soon enough; best not to encourage any thought in that direction. And yet, as we look down the road, there are going to be regrets, anger, disappointment, panic and probably fear. But what if you could change that by starting now? I believe that when death comes, if we have lived our life as fully and richly as we always wanted, if we have experienced all we want to, and if we have made bold moves, then we will not mind the going so much. And if we add to that list a strong belief in the hereafter, a strong spiritual center, it will be even less fearful. If we take care of our health, in all areas of the six dimensions, we can prolong both the number and the quality of the years we have in this body. This will give us the opportunity to fulfill all the promises of life.

When I was a young girl, I had an Aunt Mame. At the age of sixty-five, she was diagnosed with terminal cancer. She was very angry. Even at my young age, I knew why she was angry. She wasn't angry because she was going to die. She was angry because she had never lived. This woman had never married; never had a child nor a boyfriend; never traveled outside of the county she lived in; and still dwelled in the same house in which she was born, her parent's home. I found it one of the saddest stories I'd ever heard.

A well-known actor from the 1950s, George Sanders, committed suicide at the end of many years of a successful career. He left a note that contained only two words, "I'm bored." I found that one of the saddest commentaries on a human's life. Here was an individual who had fame and fortune, things that most people would love to have achieved. He had the opportunity to experience everything he could have ever wanted, and apparently did. And yet, there was something missing from his makeup. And that something caused him to be remembered more for a suicide note than for his achievements.

We all experience moments of disappointment and restlessness. But the world contains endless sources of stimulation. If I lived to 500 years, I doubt if I could ever experience everything I want to. There is always good food —you can't possibly eat everything there is—more books, more movies, more friends, more places to travel to, and a thousand and one experiences waiting for you. Unless you genuinely don't want it, there is no excuse for not living a rewarding life filled with endless riches.

I have an adopted mother whom I love very much. Her name is Lela. She was my mother's best friend and after my mother died, she stepped in to be my new mother. Her own daughter had died of a brain tumor at the age of three. She never got over it. Her only other child, a son, had fallen from a line pole at the age of eighteen, leaving him paralyzed from the waist down. The one great love of Lela's life, Don, had died an agonizing death from asthma at the young age of 50. She had borne her losses with courage and was the most gracious human I'd ever known. At the age of 87, she began losing her memory and the family put her in a nursing home. When I last saw her, she had slipped into a silent world, recognizing almost no one, including myself. My grief was overwhelming. I needed to deal with it as the lack of my every-other-week calls to her had left an enormous hole. Not being able to share confidences with her nor hear for the thousandth time the story of her life and the wisdom she had garnished from it was devastating. It was as if she were already dead, although I knew that when her body followed suit, I would have to grieve all over.

I thought a lot about her life, about the sensitive and caring human she had become. I pictured myself going through such painful times as she had and began to see that Lela had chosen for herself the best way to deal with years of pain. She knew her life was coming to an end and the pictures in her mind had been looked at so often with so many tears that now she wanted peace. No matter how much she might wish it, her body would not drop until it was ready, and so she decided to find her peace now. Coming to this conclusion helped me deal with my own world of pain. I like to think that we humans have the ability to choose wherever we want to go whether it be financially, socially, physically, spiritually, emotionally, or, especially, mentally. In my mind, Lela's silent world is a gentle, soothing place, one where she experiences only serenity. I can let go of the pain, knowing she too is able to do the same.

Picture yourself at the age of ninety-five. Your hearing is getting worse; your eyesight is failing; you can't climb mountains anymore; and when you travel, you have dizzy spells. You've taken good care of your body up until now and it has served you well. You know it's normal for your organs and senses to be failing. You've acquired wisdom and inner peace; you've traveled every place you want to go; had many years of wedded bliss with the person you love; you've raised children of whom you're very proud; seen them raise their children and their children's children. You've laughed; you've made wonderful friends; you've learned everything you had a thirst for. Your whole life has been a testimony to joy and rewards. You've followed through on every dream and seen it to fruition. You've worked on finding a belief in the after-life. You're fully convinced from all you've read as well as personal experiences, where loved ones from the other side have contacted you, that once you drop your body, your soul will join others that have already left and that you miss so much. You are totally convinced that awareness exists after death that connects you to your current lifetime. Most importantly, you have a strong belief in God and are in daily communication with him.

But you're tired and it's time to drop your body.

Gently, one night, with your loved one's hand in yours, you let go of your body in your sleep and find yourself entering a magical realm. The feeling of weightlessness is marvelous. You discover that awareness and a reality exist on the other side of the body that is even more than you'd ever hoped for. A sense of total happiness is now forever yours.

Not bad?

What if you could control this picture and make it a reality for you?

	Making Every Moment Count

In line with the previous chapter is the knowledge that a rewarding life means making every moment count. Even the quiet, peaceful moments in life count. All of our senses are gifts, glorious rewards for being born. With our eyes, we see sunsets, mountains, our grandchildren, read books, and watch movies. Our ears are tools to hear music, words, the sound of crickets, and so on. Our taste buds bring endless satisfaction and the ability to smell every fragrance and every type of food is yet another type of joy. Hugs, kisses, body massages, hand holding, and a healthy sex life with someone you love contain even more deeply satisfying moments. A thousand times we have the ability to utilize all of these senses.

And yet, how many pleasures have we missed with our distractions? We drive up the coastline of California, thinking about a business deal we're headed for and how best to make it work. Do we notice the many colors in the Pacific Ocean and how they change over and over as we head north? Do we smell the sea breeze and marvel at how it can fill all the corners in our mind? Are we listening to Rhapsody in Blue by George Gershwin, one of the most beautiful pieces of music ever written? Or are we only listening to the noise in our mind?

Every moment in our life contains so much more than we are paying attention to. When I lived in the Colorado Rockies and stepped out on our back deck, I could have done two things. I could have taken a surface look to see what the weather might be and head back inside. Or I could have taken a few moments and breathed deeply of the pine trees, watched an Albert's squirrel scamper up a tree as he headed for our bird feeder, felt the warmth of the mountain sun on my arms, and heard the sound of the summer breeze as it explored the limbs of trees in its journey. One of those moments was more deeply satisfying than the other.

I love to cook. I can throw a hamburger on the grill and enjoy it immensely or I can spend an hour creating an entirely new dish, experimenting with this season and that, even reading up on the spices as I cook. If someone asked me at this moment what I was reading, my answer would be: *Canterbury Tales, Lincoln: An Illustrated Biography*, Dante's *Divine Comedy, Dark History of the Kings and Queens of England, The Great Book of World Heritage Sites, Caesar and Christ* by Will Durant, the *Great Triumvirate, Unholy Alliance, The Bible* (second time), *The Praise of Folly, Thomas More, Greatness to Spare*, and the *7 Habits of Highly Effective People*. I usually read 12 to 15 books at a time and am fortunate to have a multi-track mind and can keep each book separate reading whichever one my current mood requires. Being able to do this enriches my life.

My husband is an expert power lounger and takes great pride in this. I am happiest when my days are filled with both pleasure and purpose. Tom is forever saying, "Come sit on the back deck with me." I can do this for a while. But eventually, I need to attend to my purpose whether it is getting household chores done, practicing piano or guitar, taking a walk, or working on a manuscript. I am fortunate that I find pleasure in my purpose but, to me, accomplishing goals gives my life meaning.

How many elderly people start their conversations with "If only I'd gone to college", or "If only I'd followed my instincts in choosing my mate in life", or "I always wanted to climb mountains, if only I'd done that when I was younger" etc. Why must people wait until it's too late to make every moment count?

It is said that on one's deathbed, the main thing one regrets is not making bold moves. I find that to be true in my own life, specifically in two incidents. The first was when my second husband wanted a divorce. He always got rid of wives and pets when they were no longer obedient. I had made the mistake of being disobedient. He and I had spent almost ten years building up a large corporation, beginning with three employees and ending up with almost 200 at the time of the divorce. I had started out alongside him by doing the bookkeeping, finally learning accounting and pulling a Profit and Loss statement every month. I had gone on to become the Sales Manager, managing seven sales reps across the country. I also was the Office Manager with three people working in the office. There was little, with the exception of manufacturing, that I didn't know about the business, including shipping and receiving and fabrication. During most of those years, my husband was an alcoholic, coming in to work at 9:00 and leaving at 11:00 for lunch (and the bars), not returning home till 2:30 in the morning. I covered for him and made sure everything ran smoothly. I had 2500 customers in my head, their purchasing agents, the volume of sales they did as well as what products they purchased

When it came time for the property settlement, I told my attorney to ask for half of the business. My husband went in to a rage and insisted that I was getting nothing. I ignored him. Finally, he informed me that he had access to the highest paid and most successful attorneys in the Los Angeles area and that if I tried to take any part of our business, he would make sure that I was proven an unfit mother and my children were taken away from me. I knew that, despite failings in other areas, I was a good mother, active in community affairs and their scouting and sports activities, a part-time volunteer teacher's aide, and a hands-on mother who read to them, helped them with their homework, handled their character development, and hosted more slumber and holiday parties (including one for my son's football team) than any other mother. The idea that my husband could take my children from me seemed ridiculous.

My first husband (the father of the children), from whom I'd been divorced for over ten years, found out I was getting a divorce from my second husband and decided it was time for me to come home. When I refused (he had been an abusive alcoholic —adults who have a childhood sexual abuse background tend to pick more than one abuser), he began daily death threats, saying he would have a shotgun pointed at my head when I walked out the door after work and would pull the trigger. I became terrified and finally called the police. After listening in to one of my many-times-a-day calls, they met me at the front door every evening with guns drawn, searched the grounds and escorted me to my home, then inside it. This went on for weeks. With one ex husband handing out daily death threats and another soon-to-be-ex threatening to take my children away, I finally folded and let my current husband have all of the business and all of our assets. This was over 24 years ago and the amount of money my half would be worth millions today. I would never have had to work again. I would have had the funds to send my children to college and live life the way I wanted to. I've regretted it ever since. If only I'd had a stout heart, the courage to make bold moves. But that was before I'd gone into recovery and found out that I did have the courage inside of me to combat that kind of abuse.

The second time was when my younger sister, Jeanne, was in a car accident at the age of 25. My mother, worn down from raising four other children, had turned her over to me. I had raised her from the time of her birth when I was only nine years old, getting up in the middle of the night to give her a bottle and change her diapers, vacuuming with her on my hip, and forgoing any normal childhood activities so that I could be with Jeanne. I loved her more than I could possibly describe. As she grew older, she became not only my child and my sister, but also my best friend. In the car accident, her abdomen hit the steering wheel of her Volkswagen when a woman ran a stop sign. Jeanne's liver had been torn in three places. The injuries were severe and after surgery my brother Scott and I headed for Intensive Care to see her.

Several months earlier Jeanne had called to talk to me about a matter of great importance to her. Her psychic powers had been considerable and, despite being happily married and in the middle of writing an exciting book, she told me her life was soon to end and she wanted to tell me how to prepare her funeral. She had also sent me a letter describing all of this in detail and saying she was 'coming to the ages'. As Scott and I walked towards Intensive Care, this was all I thought of. We turned a corner and I saw a fuzzy picture of my sister in the hospital bed, swathed in bandages with tubes and monitors hooked up to her body. My mind filled with terror and I ran smack into a wall, slithered to the ground and lay there, too frightened to get up and walk the last few steps to see my baby sister. My brother helped me up and stated that we would go see her later. Later never came. She died without either of us saying goodbye. I've regretted that for over thirty years. If only I'd had the courage.

One of my favorite lines is from a movie called *Cousins* (1989). In it, the character played by Ted Danson has an uncle who makes a comment about him: "Larry has failed in every-thing but life." What a great philosophy! It's okay to fail as long as you're enjoying whatever it is you're doing. In fact, failure is a part of life. There is no shame in it at all. The list of Abraham Lincoln's failures before he finally succeeded is so long that you'd be shocked, thinking no one who had that many failures could have ever succeed in anything. Larry, the character in the movie, had the marvelous ability to be spontaneous, playful, to laugh at his own foibles and mistakes, and especially to find joy in everything he did. He was the kind of person everyone wants to be around. He made every moment count. What a talent!

If you had only one year to live, what would your choices be? Few people ask themselves that because they don't want to think about the possibility of their life ending. It's a question one hears frequently, but most people don't actually ever have to face it. Would you change nothing? If that's true, then you are no doubt living exactly the way you want to. What a blessing! But if a hundred changes come to your mind, then it's time to make those changes now. Don't wait till a death sentence is your carrot.

10 Mental Dimension

Let's start the creation of our perfect world with the first dimension on my list—mental. This includes all areas that have to do with the mind: communication—whether it be talking, writing, reading, listening, or thinking—and any intellectual responses relating to external activity. Since your mind is the director of that movie you call your life, wisdom dictates that you have the best available. If I had to list five rules in the area of the mental dimension that promote good mental health, they would be as follows:

- Promote good mental stimulation in a variety of areas through books, movies, the Internet, good conversation, travel etc.
- Strive to remain stable, centered, and purposeful.
- Use your head before you use your words, and especially before you take action.
- Develop rock solid confidence.
- Develop and nurture a positive and optimistic attitude about life.
- Life is too short to be little.
- Utilize all the properties of awareness.

Let's break these rules down and find a way to make them work.

Promote Good Mental Stimulation in a Variety of Areas

I'm not a reader, you say. I don't like the Internet and don't understand computers anyway. I hate travel and my idea of good conversation is to talk about what happened on the soaps. Whoops! If you've given these answers, you have no one but yourself to blame if you find life boring.

Life is an adventure. It need not be fearful. Perhaps you don't read because it was never encouraged in your childhood. Go to a library or a bookstore. Wander through it until a section catches your eye. Everyone is interested in something. Maybe audio-books are more your style. There's a wide variety available. You don't have to like the Internet, but perhaps you don't because you've heard negative things about it (which may or may not be true) or because it seems too complicated. The very thought of even attempting to understand it makes you feel as if your ignorance is going to show and you're not willing to let that happen. Take a chance. Find someone who uses the Internet frequently and have him or her give you a tour of what is available. I can almost guarantee you'll be hooked.

How about travel? A lot of people really don't like to travel. There's no shame in that. But have you thoroughly investigated every possibility. Maybe you're frightened of air travel but trains interest you. Perhaps getting in a car and just going to a nearby city will whet your appetite. Better yet, perhaps moving through the Internet may cause you to discover places you never knew you were interested in. Sometimes, a lack of interest is only a lack of knowledge. One of the most marvelous side effects of travel is that it stimulates interest in history, geography, geology, and a host of other things. Many people who could care less about history wound up in Gettysburg and found themselves so moved that they developed an interest in the Civil War.

Or picture this. What if you're touring an old home from the Revolutionary War in Delaware and see a spinning wheel. You've never cared for antiques before but you're looking at this as if it's a work of art. You wander off, thinking about that antique mall you passed earlier in the day. By the time you get home, you've combed bookstores and libraries for literature on antiques.

I admit that most people's conversations are somewhat trite, definitely lacking in stimulation. But what if you have a secret longing to find out about butterflies and one day you discover a group that meets at your library to go butterfly watching. It would change your life. You'd have something to not only learn, but to talk about. The joy of sharing an idea, a concept, or an interest is a wonderful experience. The mental stimulation of sharing your thoughts will encourage you to go down more and more roads. Who knows? From there, you may wind up wanting to go back to school to learn about Biology.

Make a list of those things that appeal to you. It doesn't matter how silly it may appear to others. My husband is a transportation nut. He loves miniature vehicles. We have train sets, miniature airplanes, trucks, cars, motorcycles, and even antique plows that were in his family from the late 19th century. Sounds silly to you? He is enthralled, not only with his collection, but the many books he has purchased regarding them. It led him to the idea of building his own models. That led to more books on how to do that as well as books written by people who have the same interest.

Almost every time Tom and I watch a movie, it leads us to explore the Internet. We spend a great deal of time on Google and often check out a movie database web site to see the history of the making of the film and what awards it may have won. If it's a movie about a historical figure, we are curious to find out what they looked like, more about their life, how historically accurate the movie we just watched actually was, and so on. Since we have a library of over 8,000 books, this thirst for knowledge heads us up to the third floor library to look up even more. This leads to fascinating conversations on a certain era, a world event, or even another famous person. To date, we have found absolutely nothing that we type in "Google" that doesn't produce a wealth of information, from famous quotes to famous people, to famous events and famous places. Even some not-so-famous show up. I typed in my hometown one time, a village of 380 people and guess what? There was a web site for Petersburg, Nebraska. Because of our continuing curiosity, there is no lack of mental stimulation in our house.

Keep in mind that one thing leads to another. You need only follow the thread and see what journeys you will embark on. A few minutes of watching the news may cause your previously undeveloped interest in China to prompt you to look up the country on the Internet. While paging through various links you see one on the Great Wall. You've never thought of the Great Wall before but now when you view photos and read the history, you find your mind has traveled to the Orient and all of a sudden, you, who never liked to travel, want your body to follow.

Some of you pessimists are saying. Fine for you to say all of this. You can probably afford to travel and buy antiques. It's all I can do to pay my bills.

Guess what? I told you that you never know where a thread is going to lead you. It costs nothing to go to a library. Maybe while you're there, you see a sign asking for part-time workers. It doesn't pay much but after some inquiries you find out they're willing to train you on the computer and on your breaks, you can surf the Internet. By the end of your first week of work, you've not only got a few extra dollars in your pocket, you've made some new friends (one of them has a brother that has his own business and is looking for someone with your talents to come to work for him for double what you're making now), you've learned a lot about computers and the Internet and, wonder of wonders, you had no idea you were interested in gems and minerals. By the end of the month, you've organized a hike out to a local mine with some friends of yours to look for rocks and minerals. You discover there's a local gem and mineral club and they're looking for new members. In the space of a few weeks, your whole life has changed. The mental stimulation you've acquired alone is worth the trip to the library.

Strive to Remain Stable, Centered, and Purposeful

We all suffer from melancholy in varying degrees and varying amounts. Many choices lie in front of you to rid yourself of melancholy. If it's not that often, it may not be a bad thing. I find that every once in a while, indulging in sadness at different losses and worries is even good for me. We all need "sulking" time. As long as you don't encourage it for all it's worth and don't ruin other people's day with it, it's okay. Feelings just are, and being in touch with them, no matter what they are, promote our well-being. Sit and have sad thoughts if you need to; then put them away and go on with your life. An episode of healing happens when we sit and feel our sadness. Working through it puts it to rest.

But if it's chronic sadness, it needs attention. Are you getting enough sleep? I'm convinced that the majority of suicides are committed by people who've been plagued with insomnia. In a later chapter, we'll deal with insomnia and some solutions. Are you eating a healthy diet? I'm talking about no junk food; easy on the caffeine, the sugar, and the processed foods. Eat lots of fruits and vegetables, rice and beans, as little red meat as possible, and drink lots of water. Get a copy of the Food Pyramid and use it as your guide (type in "Food Pyramid" on Google). If you don't believe that eating healthy contributes to your well-being, try eating junk food for one week and then healthy food for another. You'll see the difference. I mentioned this once before in my *REPAIR* manual, but it bears repeating.

Feeling centered is an important part of living. Take a few minutes each day to sit quietly and do nothing. Let your mind roam and relax. Feel the center of your being. Go there and visit. This will contribute a great deal to your mental well-being. Transcendental Meditation is another way to relax and feel centered. You can pay hundreds of dollars to take a course on it (which I did) or you can follow a few simple rules and teach yourself. All it takes is 20 minutes twice a day. Sit yogi style, take several deep breaths, clear your mind of all thoughts, and then gently repeat a mantra over and over. A mantra is nothing more than a meaningless sound. For example: *ooohm* is a meaningless sound. Make up one of your own. Just be sure to use the same one each time you meditate. As you repeat this meaningless sound, you will find your mind wandering to problems and future events. Gently push them away and keep repeating your meaningless sound. At the end of the twenty minutes, you will feel refreshed and peaceful.

Feeling purposeful may be a bit more difficult. It requires goal-setting. They may be large goals or they may be small. Attending college is a large goal that causes you to feel purposeful on a daily basis. Planning an evening's meal may be a smaller goal but is no less important in your life. Think about what you like to do best. If you like plants, then working in a garden or doing yard work at the end of your day, or on a weekend, may be a small part of your purpose.

When I first moved to Colorado, I realized our three and a quarter acres was a wealth of creativity that made me feel purposeful. I began gathering stumps that looked like parts to a set on a movie about wizards. I organized them in an artistic fashion in the center of three pine trees. I then placed river rock between each stump as a ground cover. It looked marvelous. I also dug a trench, a rock river bed that ran about a dozen yards down to a rock pond at the bottom. In the center, I placed a Japanese style chipmunk bridge. Not only did it make me feel purposeful, it was great cardiovascular exercise and the only money required was for the bridge. I found the rocks that I used for the border as well as the multi-colored stones for the bed on our property.

If you enjoy your job, then doing the best you can at it on a daily basis will be another way of feeling purposeful. If you're family-oriented and plan activities for them, there's another purpose. The world is full of choices that can make you feel purposeful. If your only goal on a daily basis is to stumble through your day, hoping nothing bad happens, that is not purposeful.

Make a list of all the things you enjoy. How many of them are you actually involved in? How about goals? Surely there are things you've always wanted to accomplish. No time like the present to start. Working towards goals provides two good mental health dimensions. One, it stimulates your enjoyment of and participation in life. Two, it keeps your mind off other things that may be bothering you.

Another important word about good mental health. Much has been said about staying in present time. I discovered one day that I was subject to various triggers throughout the day that catapulted me back to an unpleasant event from a previous time. This is true of all of us but I appeared to be doing what I refer to as "connecting the dots". I noticed that if my husband mentioned a place he'd been before, in my mind, I wasn't living in the current story he was telling. Rather I was assuming that he too "connected the dots." A story about his life in St. Louis (where he lived for a year with his ex-wife, an extremely unpleasant person) was not just about the St. Louis incident. I thought he was dwelling on his life with his ex-wife, the pain he suffered in the aftermath of the divorce, and so on. Since he brought it up so often, I felt it was detrimental to our relationship that he was unable to let go of his relationship with her. When I mentioned this to him, he was amazed. The only thing on his mind was the story he was telling. Not so if it had been me. If he mentioned Bob Dylan, I didn't just think about the singer, I recalled the man I was dating at the time and how much cheating and drugs and drinking happened during that era and how abusive and unkind the man had been. I very swiftly began a spiral of sadness when all Tom had done was mention Bob Dylan.

Once I realized that a large part of my mental imaging consisted of connecting the dots, that is, this reminded me of that; that reminded me of this; and so on, till my mind was a labyrinth of unpleasantness from my past. It was much easier for me to concentrate on what was at hand, the present moment only. It's easy to say that the past is gone and the future is not here so why live anywhere but in the present and much harder to follow through on it. Once you recognize that you are creating your own unpleasantness, and that if you wish to change the tide of the future you must use the wisdom you are able to gather from the present, life becomes simpler and your mental health much better.

Putting your attention on problems simply to mentally masturbate isn't healthy. Working towards resolving them is. Little good has ever come out of anyone sitting around and feeling sorry for themselves. Take action! Make your life happen! Begin with good mental health.

Use Your Head Before You Use Your Words or Take Action

Not saying anything is sometimes better than not thinking before speaking. Thinking things through first buys one time to make a choice on what you want your words to be. This is a lot harder for some of us to put in practice than one would think. Those of you who are listeners, have a methodical as opposed to an impulsive nature, and always plot your course in life, might have an easier time with it. For those of you who are not so blessed, using your head will take practice.

How many times have you said something and later regretted it, you know, *open mouth, insert foot?* I remember an incident when I was in high school. A nice young lady named Pam was in my class. When I was introduced to her I blurted out, "Did you know one of your eyes is higher than the other?" The look of dismay on her face caused me to feel instant shame at my own insensitivity. I'm not an insensitive person by nature and had no idea why I said such a cruel thing. The next day when I saw her I noticed that she walked with her head cocked as if trying to even her eyes out. I never saw her again when she didn't have her head cocked. It has bothered me ever since and I wish I could contact her to say how sorry I am.

I've done the same thing more than once, maybe not told someone his or her eyes were crooked, but said something without thinking. Time has taught me to temper such a character trait but I still need to work on it. One thing I learned that helped a great deal was when I realized that people who are verbal by nature are more inclined to say things without thinking first. That made me realize that others who appear to be more sensitive may just have the good sense to keep their mouths shut. Being open is usually perceived as a good thing. And it may well be. But it still needs to be accompanied by common sense.

If you think you can get in trouble by speaking without thinking, acting without thinking can be even worse. Unless you work in an Emergency Room or are a fireman, few occurrences throughout your day need an immediate response. I've been listening lately to a set of audiotapes on the Civil War. I've learned that some of the generals, George McClellan for example, were brilliant soldiers and strategists, but did not know how to press forward when they had the advantage. Still others, such as Ulysses S. Grant, moved immediately when it was time to strike. A soldier in war has a different scenario than a civilian. Ultimately, it all comes back to common sense. Some events require thinking through first and others require spontaneity and impulsivity. Knowing the difference and acting accordingly is where your power lies.

Keep in mind that some actions promote results that cannot be overturned, ever.

I have a wonderful son-in-law named Larry. When he was in his early twenties, he and a friend had been at the Colorado River on a gambling trip. They decided to drive upriver to another casino. Having not slept in many hours, both were tired. Larry, always a methodical thinker, told his friend he thought they should get some sleep and not try to drive any further. The friend, who was doing the driving, disagreed; so off they went. Larry fell asleep. So did his friend. Larry woke to oncoming headlights, saw they were in the wrong lane and grabbing the steering wheel, yanked them into their own lane and safety. His friend woke up, startled, and Larry again told him they must stop and get some sleep. The friend insisted the incident had scared him bad enough. He was wide-awake now and there was no need to stop. Larry didn't agree but again was overruled. Within minutes Larry again fell asleep and so did his friend. This time when Larry woke to oncoming headlights, it was too late. His friend was killed and Larry is a quadriplegic. I wonder how many times Larry has said to himself, "if only…"

Never doubt that your inner voices are constantly at work, telling you what is the best thing to do. Ignoring your intuition can be costly.

Develop Rock Solid Confidence

What a challenge this is! It's been especially so with me because of the severity of my abuse in both my childhood and in ensuing relationships in my adult years. Even after recovery, it's been difficult. It's something I practice every day. People who suffered abuse in their childhood are subject to periodic triggers. These are events in our current life that set off memories we thought we had long ago addressed and healed. Not only do they usually happen unexpectedly, but also we are not always aware of their existence. If you find yourself becoming disturbed or anxious out of proportion at something that is happening, stop and take a few minutes to think about it rather than impulsively responding. Did a similar occurrence happen in your childhood or in your previous life that frightened you?

When Tom and I were first married, I asked him to change a light bulb. He became very angry, slamming doors, banging his fist on walls, and muttering obscenities to himself. I became frightened immediately and it escalated beyond what either of us had anticipated. After we both calmed down and talked about it, we discovered that his actions had triggered painful events I had lived through with abusive husbands. Tom, on the other hand, had been previously married to a highly controlling woman and, despite the many years since his divorce, didn't take kindly to any requests. Tom is by nature a gentle and kind human being. He was appalled at his own behavior and apologized. We worked through it and today I don't even have to ask him to change a light bulb. He does it immediately.

Watch for triggers, expect them, and deal with them by going to a quiet place and locating their source. Take current events and place them in the proper perspective. If these happen in a relationship, dialoguing about them helps a great deal. Never be afraid to talk openly about what you're feeling and thinking with a trusted friend or loved one. It accomplishes two things. One, you've taken steps to resolving a problem; and two, you've improved your self-esteem.

Go back to Chapter Two and re-read the tips on improving your self-esteem. This entire book is designed to empower you and developing confidence is about just that.

It's also about knowing you're going to be all right no matter what happens. I've found that the most attractive quality I've ever seen in a person is confidence. I've known people who would otherwise never be noticed, because they are not particularly attractive, become head turners because of their self-confidence. On the flip side, I've seen people who are gorgeous but who become unattractive because of their lack of confidence.

A few years ago, I was in England at a place called Hampton Court. It was one of Henry VIII's palaces and had a world-famous maze in its lovely gardens. For those who don't know what a maze is, it's a tall hedge that grows in such a way that it covers a large portion of land and has intricate paths that twist and turn. Once you enter it, it is very difficult to find your way out and a good number of people had entered it only to discover that finding their way out was much more difficult than they had thought.

It had been said that Henry VIII had designed it on purpose so that he could trap potential (and unwilling) mistresses in it. I entered it with total confidence along with several other tourists. There was no way I was going to get lost or panic-stricken here. Within a few minutes I found myself somewhat nervous. Let's see was it left or right at this junction? Surely I've already passed this part of the maze. I soon decided that this was no fun and, trying to ignore my growing anxiety, I decided, "I'm getting out of here." To my surprise, I couldn't find my way out. I passed various people who had the same stunned and anxious look on their faces that I had. I began feeling claustrophobic and every twist and turn made me think I was going deeper and deeper into terror. I pictured having to stay here forever and when I heard shouts of "Help, I can't find my way out," it only contributed to my sense of growing panic. Coming from a place of fear literally removed all my confidence. There is little room in your mind for both fear and confidence.

Of course, eventually I did find my way out. It took a while and I was extremely grateful to finally find the exit. I realized that there had been signs posted there that said if you can't find your way out, just shout and someone will guide you. What I learned about this rather silly experience was that had I reminded myself all along that no matter what happened I was going to be fine, I would have had no sense of panic, only a sense of adventure. That encouraged me to do a lot of thinking about confidence and about how knowing you're going to be all right no matter what plays a large part in developing your own.

What if you told yourself that exact thing—that no matter what happened, you were going to be all right? How would that make your life different? When I was in recovery, one of my many therapists had taught me a game he and his family played. Whenever one of his children brought up a particular problem at the dinner table, he would say, "And?" This would encourage them to find another way around the problem. There are various interpretations of this theme —a niece of mine is prone to saying (when people begin whining about their problems) "and your problem is?" This is a somewhat rude version of the same game. But it does cause you to stop and think about how much of a martyr in your day-to-day life you really are.

Let's take an example. You have a job interview. You really, really want this job. You not only want this job, you need it. Your whole life depends on it. So you get yourself fixed up in your best Sunday outfit and head out the door for the company that is the object of your heart's desire. You're on time, but somewhat nervous. Perhaps you didn't sleep well. Your anxiety increases the closer you get. How about stopping at a parking lot, take a deep breath, and begin asking yourself some questions. "What if I don't get this job?" Your response, "And?" should cause you to breathe easier. Your answer, "I'll have to stay where I am," your response again; "And?" makes you breathe easier again. Your response, "But I don't like it there" brings another "And?" "I guess I'll have to look for another job," brings another "And?" and so on. We all think that if something we want in life isn't going to happen, then the next step is the worst case scenario, maybe even death. That's it; we'll probably die if we don't get this or that. The truth is you will not die and your worst case scenario will probably not happen and even if it does, so what?

There's always another choice and maybe not getting this job will be one of the best things that happened. All you need is to keep pulling yourself back to the reality of what is happening. You are not going to die; you are not going to be living in a homeless shelter; you are only not going to get a job you had your heart set on. It certainly does not mean you don't have a better job waiting for you. It only means it's not this one. Just keep reminding yourself that no matter what happens, you are going to be okay. And you almost certainly will. A very wise, elderly Austrian woman told me one time I should always say to myself, "This or better." This philosophy has helped me accept many disappointments. As a rule, they usually turn out to be for the best.

Sometimes it helps to think back on what you have been through already. If a multitude of traumatizing events have occurred in your life, it might be normal for you to automatically think negative thoughts about the current event. On the other hand, if you think back to those things that you feared the most, the majority probably never happened.

Develop and Nurture a Positive and Optimistic Attitude

For some, this comes easier than others. Melancholy people, pessimists, are often that way by nature. I used to say that my father lived on the dark side of the moon. No matter what happened, he always looked at the down side. It was almost as if, in our household, it was wrong to feel optimistic about something. By nature, I was an optimist, a Pollyanna. We all know Pollyannas who just can't resist being, like Nellie in *South Pacific*, a cock-eyed optimist. But when you're feeling down over something, it can be tough to pull out of it. Negative energy weighs more than positive energy and if you don't feel good about your life or how it's going, it's pretty easy to look only on the dark side. One can almost get angry with those who want us to look at the bright side. "It's easy for them to say," we state, feeling resentful at their optimism since it so difficult for us to do the same. How do we pull out of that behavior pattern?

First of all, recognize that your attitude is a behavior pattern. As such, it can be changed. All it takes is willingness. It doesn't happen overnight. Sometimes it feels like the old story of the chicken and the egg. Which came first? If only we had confidence, we could have a positive attitude. And if only we had a positive attitude, we could develop confidence. Go back and re-read the part in Chapter Two on developing self-esteem. Get to work. Once you do this, developing a positive attitude will come easy.

Most people have dark times that they don't understand. This is a part of both the emotional and mental dimension but we will address it here first since your thoughts are so much a source of your emotions. Your life may be working well; you have a good job, a happy family, lots of interests, good health, and so on. But for reasons not understandable, you periodically fall into a black hole with no idea why or what is bothering you. Sometimes, quiet contemplation can locate the answer and sometimes it's just a matter of wading through it and saying "This too shall pass." Not all sad times need an explanation. Sometimes they just are! Winston Churchill, a man the world over views as being successful in all aspects of his life, was subject to frequent dark moods. He called them "black dogs" and merely waited until they passed.

Being depressed needn't hamper you. Another famous man, Abraham Lincoln, suffered most of his life from something called melancholia, a manic-depressive psychosis. At times, it was so severe that he would literally take to his bed for months on end. And this was before the death of his two sons and the heavy burden of the Civil War. And yet, that same man found the courage, the strength and the optimism to hold a nation together during a time when it was hemorrhaging from massive and internal wounds of the spirit; a man who, before he was savagely murdered, had the nobility to "with malice towards none" direct that same nation to bind up its wounds with forgiveness.

Life is Too Short to Be Little.

While this should be self explanatory, I'm going to elaborate by quoting Benjamin Disraeli, the great British Prime Minister. He said:

> "Often we allow ourselves to be upset by small things we should despise and forget. Perhaps some man we helped has proved ungrateful.....some woman we believed to be a friend has spoken ill of us....some reward we thought we deserved has been denied us. We feel such disappointments so strongly that we can no longer work or sleep. But isn't that absurd? Here we are on this earth with only a few more decades to live and we lose many irreplaceable hours brooding over grievances that in a year's time will be forgotten by us and by everybody. No, let us devote our life to worthwhile actions and feelings, to great thoughts, real affections, and enduring undertakings. Life is too short to be little."

Give it a try and you'll see how much better you feel.

Utilize All the Properties of Awareness.

Awareness has many properties. Each one can contribute to our mental well being. They include:

- *Sensibility* is the capacity to reason, to use your head and think things through.
- *Prudence* is cautious, not headstrong or impulsive; uses reason to discipline itself and once disciplined, sees life fall into order rather than chaos.

- *Knowledge* gathers experiences and sorts through them for the right answers.
- *Visualization* is the ability to see all that you know, bringing it to life so that you can choose your next step.
- *Foresight* takes us from the past to the present and into the future.

The existence of human frailty dictates that we use understanding in our daily lives, not only our own but others, for understanding is the key and acceptance is the door. Sometimes out of the deepest of our sorrows rise the greatest of our character traits and our strength. Never underestimate the importance of stalwartly moving through a difficulty that seems insurmountable. For it may be that this very sadness and depression, like a seed casually thrown onto rocky soil that produces the loveliest of blossoms, will be responsible for molding a quality we thought lay dormant within us, transform-ing us into a noble human being, a goal we previously thought unattainable. From your very thoughts, grow the actions that will govern the success or failure of your life.

11 | Emotional Dimension

Emotional well-being is more important than any of the other six dimensions. If your emotions are out of whack—depression, lethargy, melancholy, sitting on the pity pot, and so on—you're not going to be in shape to make wise decisions in any of the other six dimensions. It's important that you *feel* good about life. From that base you, can accomplish everything you want to.

If I had to list eight rules in the area of our emotional dimension that promote good emotional health, they would be as follows:

- Work through grief, anger, and disappointment of any childhood traumas in a disciplined and positive manner.
- Find ways to feel wonder, joy, and enchantment in your universe on a daily basis.
- Remember that you're in charge of your own emotions.
- Learn to respond, not react.
- Spend quality time with both things you love and people you love.
- Practice forgiveness on a daily basis.
- Remember, "Understanding is the key, acceptance is the door".

- If you can't say something nice, don't say anything at all.

Let's break these rules down and find a way to make them work.

Work Through Grief, Anger, and Disappointment

This does not have to be that difficult. Working through childhood traumas, getting into a recovery program, or letting go of past hurts has been dealt with to some degree already. Once you do this, you'll find that there are still days when things don't go as you want them. There will still be hurts and disappointments to rear their ugly heads. This is all a part of life and no one escapes unscathed. It's how you deal with them that matters. Mostly, it just takes a positive attitude.

A while ago, when I was scheduled to teach seminars on my REPAIR program, a program I had developed for recovery from childhood sexual abuse, I was working with a leading Health Maintenance Organization (HMO) in the San Diego area. Their Health Education Department was involved with the Centers for Disease Control in Atlanta, Georgia, in a survey that went out to seventeen thousand members of the HMO. The questions on the survey had to do with the correlation between childhood traumas and adult onset health disorders. The results produced amazing data. Childhood abuse, neglect, and exposure to other traumatic stressors, which they termed "adverse childhood experiences" (ACE), were common. Almost two-thirds of their study participants reported at least one ACE, and more than one in five reported three or more ACE. The short- and long-term outcomes of these childhood exposures included a multitude of health and social problems. This, more than anything else, led me to believe that the inter-connectedness of at least the emotional, mental, and physical dimensions was extremely strong. It was a short hop to realizing that all six were connected.

I discovered a rather simple three-step way to deal with posttraumatic stress. At least it's simple in so far as the steps, but each step may entail hard work and courage.

I have a brother I love a great deal who served as a medical corpsman for many years in Vietnam. He saw horrors so unbelievable that he still can't bring himself to talk about them. Ever since those years, he has been an alcoholic. Periodically he tried to stop drinking with half-hearted programs, never acknowledging the root of the trauma that caused him to become an alcoholic.

I'm convinced that most people who have addictions come from a place of deep sorrow over something. It may be child-hood trauma, severe grief over the loss of a loved one, sadness at being unloved or alone, or anything that puts a heavy burden on your heart. The only way to not have to feel that pain is to distract yourself with whatever your drug of choice is. Even being a workaholic is a drug of choice if it keeps us from experiencing a joyful life. Recently, after he had stopped drinking for many months, Brian again started. He also stopped his weekly phone calls to me. I knew the reason and continued to call him on a regular basis, ignoring his slurred words and periodic bouts of rage. If there was anything I had learned in life, it was that trying to control someone else's behavior never works. Unless it is their decision to take the steps to make a change, it will never hold. I had enough trouble controlling my own life anyway.

One day, I received a letter from Brian saying that he had checked himself into a rehabilitation center and they had diagnosed him as having post-Vietnam stress. He was trying to work through what had happened to him by regular counseling, church, and Twelve Step programs. He had again quit drinking and was hopeful of a complete recovery. I sent him a letter, telling him that I felt it took certain steps to arrive at complete recovery. They consist of three simple words: Real, feel, and heal. Let's break these down to more understandable terms.

Real

When the root of your sorrow is a trauma that you've never acknowledged, how can you ever recover from it? Lions and tigers and bears hiding under the bed need to be dragged out and confronted. If you keep telling yourself they aren't under there, they'll never go away. On the other hand, if you look under the bed and find there really aren't any, then your relief is immediate. But first you have to look.

I've known many a victim of child abuse that has never gone beyond their pain because they have never acknowledged what happened to them as real. Their philosophy is, "If you don't think about it, it'll go away". No! No! No! You need to make it *REAL!* While that can be incredibly painful, the pain is something that can be moved through. Like lancing a wound that has become infected, one must see the reality of what happened, admit the role you and everyone else played in it, and once having faced that demon, you can go on to the next step. I've even had people say, "Yes my father raped me but he said it was my fault". Bullshit (excuse me to those who are offended at such earthy words, but that's exactly what it is). In making a trauma real, it is necessary to see the part that everyone played in it. That means exploring the entire truth of the matter. That's why confession is so good for the soul.

My poor brother, who, like many others, who have gone years saying, "It wasn't so bad", needed to take a hard look at all the memories and say, "It was devastating." Once he's made it real, he can go on to the next step.

Feel

Now comes the grieving. Brian needs to feel all of the pain of his experience. It is no different than going through the grieving process when someone we love dies. It may all come back to him when he has preferred to lock it in a room in his mind and never think of it again. But is that in his best interests? Since he has turned to alcoholism to cope, it is obviously not in his best interests. The more you feel all of the pain, the closer you will come to the final step.

Heal

Again, I liken these steps to lancing a wound. First you acknowledge you have a wound and that it is infected. In this case, it is a mental and emotional wound. Then, you lance the wound to get rid of the infection. That is the feeling part. Sure it hurts but fast on its heels, you will discover something very dramatic and unbelievable. You are no longer in any emotional pain. When I went through recovery from my father raping me, it was as if a thousand painful pounds had been lifted from my shoulders. I literally felt reborn. It wasn't that I felt no pain. It was the single most painful thing I have ever gone through. A thousand times I wanted to give up and go back to my old ways, pretending it never happened. The road ahead seemed so long and so dark. I wanted desperately for someone to come to my rescue and make all my pain go away. Someone did. Me. At some point in time, I began to see the proverbial light at the end of the tunnel. I could feel hope. As I moved closer and closer to the end of my recovery (I titled it the Bridge of Recovery), it was as if I had been given a "second wind" so to speak. I felt myself become stronger and more powerful and especially felt the healing taking place.

Let's look at someone who just lost his or her job. That's a heavy blow to anyone, especially if it's unexpected and it's a job you liked a great deal. Sometimes a heavy blow (such as losing your job) is a precursor to something that is much better for you. Many a person has lost their job, ended a marriage, or a relationship, or found out they had to move, only to look back later and realize it was the best thing that ever happened to them. So don't despair, just because things look bleak. Sit quietly. Assess your situation logically. See what resources are available to you.

Another useful tool is to step back and take a global view of your situation. Sometimes we are too close to something to see its reality. When all you feel is the pain of a sorrow or disappointment, it's difficult to figure out what to do or to put the matter in the right perspective. Things may not be as bad as they seem (I think there was a popular song about that in the 50s). Detach, detach, detach. Once you do that, you can empower yourself to resolve whatever challenge lies in front of you.

If you reframe the problem, it may help you to detach. Let's take a look at two different statements made by a girl who just broke up with her boyfriend: "My heart is broken, I'll never love again; what did I do wrong?" Or, "It's pretty sad and I guess I'll go through some grieving but the truth is we just weren't right for each other anyway; when the right man comes along, I'll be glad this relationship ended". What a difference! You have the choice to view yourself as either a victim or a volunteer. In one statement, you are reaffirming that you are a victim and helpless to do anything about it. It's almost guaranteed to make you miserable. In the other, based on utilizing free choice, which is all that volunteering is, you are not only viewing things objectively, but also utilizing wisdom to decide that this is not the end of the world. In short, you are empowering yourself to bounce back.

That's what life is all about, bouncing back. No one goes on this journey without disappointments, heartaches, or grief. It's how you deal with it that separates the strong from the weak, the survivors from the victims.

Barney and Halcyon, two elderly people very dear to me, lived in a small farming community in Iowa. I had known them since I was a child. They had a wonderful married life, well over

50 years. One of their sons, a childhood playmate of mine, died from heart failure when he was in his mid teens. It devastated them. The pain of the loss of their son never went away but they learned how to deal with it and were compensated by the joy of another son. When they both had severe health problems, life was again a serious challenge. Once I spoke to Halcyon on the phone and she said they had woken up that morning, looked at each other, and said, "Smile." They both knew they were coming to the end of their journey and yet they had great courage and drew on it by using a single word. Barney has since passed away and Halcyon is going about her business, saying she is eager to drop her body and see Barney again.

Now is the time to eat healthy, get lots of sleep, and exercise regularly. They are tools to help you bounce back. Avoid people who are troublesome and who put negative energy in your path. The last thing you need are friends who either encourage your depression by making you feel victimized or heap their own sad stories on you. Surround yourself with positive, uplifting people, those who have your well-being at heart, who listen sympathetically, then make suggestions as to the next step you can take.

Find Ways to Feel Wonder, Joy, and Enchantment

One of the saddest things that happen to humans is that most of us, as we grow older, lose our sense of wonder, our feelings of joy, and our ability to find enchantment. When we are children, life seems magical. We feel immune to anything bad happening to us. We have all the time in the world to appreciate every joy available, and there are many. Climbing trees, swimming in river beds, ice skating on wintery rivers, sledding down snow-covered hills, catching fireflies, playing hide and seek, reading Nancy Drew mysteries (am I dated or what?) under a willow tree while I munched on popcorn and sipped ice cold lemonade with clinking cubes are a few of my happy memories. When I was a child, even taking frozen clothes off a clothesline in the winter had a sort of magic about it. From the vantage point of an eight year old, life is truly, as Robert Louis Stevenson put it, "so full of a number of things, we really should all be happy as kings."

Even the negatives in our lives—strict parents, daily chores, school or church when we'd rather be riding our bike, or playing baseball—seem a small price to pay for all the fun waiting. We don't have to worry about finances. That's what parents are for. Ill health is for old people, not us, and the wars and famines in the world are vague and far away, part of a universe that will never touch us.

Little by little, as we move towards our final destination, we begin to lose the magic. Most of us never recapture it. How then to find it again? It seems lost forever.

Not so. There are many secrets to regaining wonder, joy, and enchantment, many ways to see the world anew as we did when we were children.

When is the last time you watched a caterpillar creep across a leaf? When is the last time you counted stars and watched for a falling one so you could make a wish? Very little of what we lost is truly gone. It needs only to be seen from our adult self but still through a child's eyes.

My maternal grandmother, whom I adored, still climbed trees in her seventies. I still turn cartwheels and (like my grandmother) will scoot up a tree whenever one is available.

Why do you feel you need to be a child to play baseball? All you need is to put your imagination to work as a stimulus. Smell the leather in your glove, feel the sensation of sliding into home plate, hear the smack of the ball as it hits a solid home run on your bat. Then find a local adult male or female ball team and get started.

How about the next time you take a walk? Don't just move your feet. Find a park, take your shoes off, and go barefoot. Feel the grass between your toes, lie on your back, and watch the clouds float by. Walk in the rain and let water run down your cheeks onto your tongue; then turn your face to the sky. Press your cheek against the bark of a tree. Snap a maple leaf off a limb and hold it to your hand seeing how like the shape of your hand it is. Go on, don't be afraid.

Part of being a child means using all your senses to the fullest. Don't worry about not being in the mood for such "silly" stuff. Once you begin, you'll forget about it being "silly" stuff. And most importantly, remember that the only thing that's the end of the world is the end of the world.

One night when I babysat two of my grandchildren, then ages eight and ten, I suggested we turn out the lights and play hide and seek. It was great fun, followed by relay races in the living room, and a grand finale where I made an attempt to levitate them. As the evening drew to a close, my grandson said, "My other grandma never does fun things like this." I thought of his other grandma and realized she was always proper, and her idea of a good time with my granddaughter was to take her for a pedicure. While I'm glad she's there for my grandchildren to give them gifts, I'm not inclined to give (their ability to be gracious and classy will no doubt come from her). I'm also grateful I inherited my grandmother's playful, childlike behavior. You're only a child once, but your ability to be playful lasts forever.

Remember that You're In Charge of Your Own Emotions.

You can choose to feel depressed and hopeless. Or you can choose to see life as a challenge. Remember that if you feed a fear, it grows. So if you focus on what happened and why did it happen to you, you'll never pull yourself out of the sadness. If you think of the possibilities that are now open to you that may not have been open before, you'll start feeling hopeful. It's all up to you. I believe it was Eleanor Roosevelt who said, "No one can make you feel inferior or hopeless without your permission".

A word here about the wonderful world of martyrdom. There is something inexplicably soothing in feeling sorry for ourselves, in recanting all the trials and tribulations that have been heaped on us in our lifetime. It encourages sympathy from all our friends; it makes us the center of attention; and best of all, it means we don't have to be accountable for the misfortune in our own lives. Step away from this picture and take another look. Who do we admire more? People who have the courage to turn their lives around even in the face of adversity or people who moan and groan about the bad breaks that keep happening to them? Most people grit their teeth when they have to listen one more time to a friend who has constant bad luck. Look at the story of Helen Keller. Never has anyone been given so many handicaps and made so much of her life.

Feeling sorry for ourselves can be a very bad habit. We want to feel optimistic and detach from whatever's happening that's keeping our lives from being joyful, but there we go again, telling our co-workers about all the car troubles we have and about our neighbor's dog that barked all night and kept us from sleeping. And did I tell you also that a check bounced and I had to pay $100 in fees? I was so angry. How can they do this to me? I mean the punishment didn't fit the crime. Brother!

Take a hard look at yourself on a daily basis. Are you a whiner? Take one day of your life and make an effort to tell no one about negative happenings in your day. Instead say only positive things. See what happens. Negative energy begets negative energy. If the gods of the universe hear us say, "Nothing good ever happens to me," or "I just know that mechanic is going to cheat me again," guess what? They send us exactly what we're expecting. It may not change overnight but keep working at it. If something negative happens to you, like getting a speeding ticket, tell yourself, "I've been speeding a lot lately. I'm sure glad I got a ticket to remind me to slow down. I could have been killed, speeding like that." I realize it makes a better story at the office to say, "That damn cop has been laying in wait for me. I bet he had a quota to fill and picking on a woman made him feel better." Whoops! If you own your own behavior, not only will it empower you but also you'll find it easier to pull out of negative behavior faster, and magic will start happening in your life.

Learn to Respond, Not React.

There's a big difference between responding and reacting. No matter what happens in your life, reacting to it is an involuntary action. It requires no thinking, no dealing with a problem wisely. A child reacts to name calling, to disappointment, to losses of any kind. They do not have the wisdom or the maturity to do much else. Responding, on the other hand, requires coming up with an answer to a problem after thinking it through. You have the right to take all the time you need to make a decision. If someone tries to bully you into doing what he or she wants, they're making a statement about themselves, not about you. A quality friend gives you permission to take time, to be methodical in your thinking. How many times have you told yourself, "If only I'd thought that one through, this wouldn't have happened."? That's what responding is all about, letting no one and nothing pull your strings or yank your chain.

Spend Quality Time with Things and People You Love

Nothing will lift your spirits faster than being with either things you love or people you love. Sometimes when you're feeling down, it's the right time to assess what's bothering you. Then you can take action to make things right in your world. If you already know and it's not the right time to make a healthy choice, then maybe feeling better about life will put things in the right perspective and enable you later to make the right choice. Times to not try to muddle through a problem are when you haven't had enough sleep, when you're hungry, when you just finished doing finances and it always puts you in a crumby mood, and so on. The best time to make a decision on a dilemma is when you are not Hungry, Angry, Lonely, or Tired (HALT).

How many times have you felt depressed or hopeless and the phone rang? Within minutes, a phone call from a friend can get you laughing or sharing and pull you away from your problems. Any distraction that's uplifting works. As a clear illustration, I want to tell you another one of my stories.

Many years ago when I was only half way through my recovery and still married to an abuser, I felt as if I had fallen so far into a black hole that the only way out was to kill myself. It was not the first time I had tried but this time I was going to succeed. When someone is suicidal, they are not thinking of killing themselves as much as they are thinking that it will be so wonderful for the emotional pain to end. I wrote a note to my children telling them how much I loved them and how I was sorry that this would be a hardship on them but I couldn't go on any longer. At the last minute, I fell to my knees, sobbing uncontrollably. All I could say over and over was, "Help me Mother of God, please help me." (I'm a Roman Catholic and we tend to pray to the Mother of God to intercede for us, not, as so many Protestants think, pray to an idol) At that moment, the phone rang and I heard my daughter's voice.

"Mom, I thought you were coming over today."

"Tammie," I said in a bare whisper, "Remember a few years ago when you said you were suicidal."

"Yes," she said in a hesitant voice.

"What did you do to pull yourself away from the blackness?"

"I took a hot shower, Mom. Why are you thinking of killing yourself?"

I started crying and couldn't stop.

"Mom, get in the car, right now and get over here. Teri's with me. We'll help you. Get in the car now, Mom or we'll get in ours and drive over there."

Somehow I found the strength to get in the car and drive the half hour to Tammie's house. Once there, my daughters surrounded me with love and let me cry and blabber to my heart's content. At one point, I whimpered, "If only I had a mother that loved me, I wouldn't be suicidal."

My youngest daughter, Teri, said, "If you'd have succeeded today in what you set out to do that would be us talking, Mom."

I got it.

Today I can hardly believe that I used to be suicidal, that I ever put my children through that. But it is a clear (and worst case scenario) illustration of how far you can be pulled back from the darkness of an abyss if you have a distraction.

If you take time to walk on the beach, read a good book, go to a movie, work on a fun project, or anything else that makes you feel better, you'll find that when you come back to the problem, you'll see it in a different light. Even if you don't have a challenge, you're working on it is still a good idea to set aside time to do fun things or be with fun people.

Whatever you do, don't spend time when you need to feel better, with people who will only make it worse. People who live in a world of negative energy themselves or who don't have a history of living healthy lives are not who you need. Find a supportive, caring friend or family member who always makes you feel better after time spent with them.

Practice forgiveness on a daily basis.

These next three suggestions will encourage you to let go of anger. Anger is incredibly detrimental to our health, in all areas. While at times, it is appropriate, such as if someone is getting ready to do bodily harm to you or someone you love, inappropriate anger is wasted energy and emotion. If you're in the local department store and need help finding something but the salespeople are busy gossiping instead of hearing your plea for direction, it's normal to get angry. But is it healthy? In the big picture, remember to choose your battles. This isn't one worth getting upset over.

Do you have people in your past who have hurt you? We all do. Maintaining anger at them is useless. If your motivation is to hurt them, you probably won't. Sometimes it's better to confront them, get it out of your system; then let it go. Forgive them for their human frailties and remember we all have some.

"Understanding is the key, acceptance is the door"

This guideline will help along with the previous one. I've had many a time when someone angered me. Once I discovered what was behind their behavior, I understood and was able to accept their shortcomings. Let me give you an example. A co-worker is always cranky. You find this disruptive to your day and make a comment to them regarding it. All of a sudden, they begin crying and confide in you that they've been having severe marital problems and it's causing insomnia. Now you understand; now you can accept. The next time they are cranky, give them a hug or say something compassionate. You'll feel better for it and so will they.

If You Can't Say Something Nice, Don't Say Anything at All.

When I was a little girl, my mother used to make this comment repeatedly. I got tired of hearing it. I look back now and realize she was handing me wisdom. Making negative statements about people in your life becomes a habit, and not a pleasant one. Any kind of negative energy is draining. We all have negative thoughts from time to time but once you put them out there by vocalizing them, you've set in motion an action and opened the door to even more negative comments. Whether you're aware of it or not, it causes depression. I find that once I'm aware I'm doing this, it's easier to substitute something pleasant instead. If I have a handyman that's padding his paycheck by lying about how long his lunch hour was, I have three choices. I can complain to my husband as the anger at being cheated festers; I can confront the handyman; or I can choose to decide that he's so good at what he does that I'll consider his extra pay a tip. Then I need to let it go.

All of the suggested rules in this chapter improve the quality of your emotional well-being but these last three go to a deeper level. Forgiveness, understanding, and saying positive words have not only a healing effect but an empowering one, empowering you to feel happy and capable no matter what's happening in your life.

<table>
<tr><td>12</td><td>**Physical Dimension**</td></tr>
</table>

Optimum physical well-being is paramount in one's life. Without it, we have no life. If I had to list seven rules in the area of our physical dimension that promote good physical health, they would be as follows:

- Practice good nutrition.
- Exercise on a daily basis.
- Have regular checkups (dental as well as physical) and practice preventive medicine.
- Promote good grooming and good hygiene.
- Avoid smoking, alcohol, and drugs.
- Get plenty of sleep.
- Listen to your own body as it speaks to you.

Let's break these rules down and find a way to make them work.

Practice Good Nutrition

When I was younger, I thought I really knew about good nutrition. So when I was raising my kids, they always got their veggies, albeit they were canned, and their fruit, ditto and wasn't Wonder bread the best kind? I made sure they got lots of protein, nice fatty hamburgers, and we always ate bacon and eggs on weekends. Nutritious cereal consisted of Lucky Charms® and whole milk was the best, as well as ice cream and pies, cakes and homemade chocolate chip cookies. After all, ice cream was a dairy product and homemade cookies had to be good for you; they were homemade.

Once my children were all raised and I took a Nutrition class as well as started working in Preventive Medicine, I was appalled. You mean pork roast and porterhouse steak weren't good sources of nutrition? Not only was I startled, I felt terribly guilty. Now that I knew what good nutrition was, I could practice it for myself but it was too late for my kids. Unfortunately, when I tried to share with them what I was learning, they gave me a blank stare and said, "What was good enough for us is good enough for our kids." At least my son, in his early thirties, started realizing what good nutrition was and changed his diet accordingly.

For those who don't know, I'll share my education in a few brief sentences. Good nutrition is at least seven to twelve fruits and vegetables a day. And this means fresh, not canned, lots of rice and beans, non-fat dairy products, and red meat sparingly. Chicken without the skin and forget the hot dogs (if you ever knew what they put in those things, you'd never eat them again anyway). I weaned myself off whole milk to 2% and it was only a hop and a skip to non-fat milk as well as non-fat cottage cheese and non-fat sour cream. I can't even bring myself to drink whole milk anymore. Instead of ice cream, I eat sherbet and lemon ices. Instead of Lay's® potato chips, I eat pretzels or reduced fat Cheez-Its®. I never even buy corn oil. Instead, I cook with extra virgin olive oil. One of my favorite dishes is tomatoes marinated in fresh basil and olive oil with salt and pepper added. Watch the salt. You don't need as much as you think and an excess of salt is highly damaging to your body. I frequently add slivered English cucumbers and purple onions along with chopped celery and a dash of vinegar. I often pass up a hot fudge sundae in exchange for this tantalizing dish.

This doesn't mean I'm religious about my diet. When traveling, I eat whatever I want, telling myself that the dreaded "C" words (calories and cholesterol) don't pertain when you're on vacation. I'm only human. My husband has very low cholesterol and eats ice cream, whole milk, and buttered popcorn, along with M&Ms®, his favorite treat. It's tough for me to never join him but I try to do it sparingly. I also drink at least eight glasses of water a day and rarely drink any alcohol or sodas. Every time I think of my cardiovascular system trying to pump nutrients through my body without the benefit of lots of water, I shudder.

The key word to veggie eating is variety. I'm fortunate to love vegetables and will buy everything from artichokes to snow peas. Tom and I both love mushrooms as well—which are very high in nutrient value—and one of our favorite dishes is angel hair pasta with mushrooms sautéed in olive oil with cracked pepper, garlic, and sweet onions. We then toss the entire mushroom dish and pasta with fresh basil and reduced fat Parmesan cheese. It's Tom's favorite dish and has almost no fat.

Almost all foods contain nutrients and if you don't eat one, you may be missing the nutrients that are special to that particular food. Experiment. Get crazy. Try every vegetable in the produce section. Create a tantalizing fruit dish on weekends varying what you put in it; one day bananas and strawberries, the next cantaloupe slices with apples, watermelon and blueberries. Tom and I also have fresh squeezed orange or grapefruit juice with our breakfast. Anything fresh is better.

One final word regarding good nutrition. You may have been a junk food fan all of your life. You may think there's no way you can ever change. Give it a chance. It's amazing how quickly your body will adapt to healthy foods and how soon it'll no longer be able to tolerate potato chips and banana splits.

Exercise on a Daily Basis

I know, I know. You're not into physical exercise. It's boring; it's a waste of time; and you're much too tired at the end of the day to do anything except prowl the Internet or watch television. Think again. Exercise does not exhaust you. It gives you energy. In addition, it releases endorphins, which create a state of euphoria. It's pretty hard to live on the dark side of the moon when you exercise regularly. Exercise is only boring if that's what you choose. And as far as a waste of time goes, if you don't exercise, you are really wasting your time because you'll no doubt die young.

There are many ways to exercise. If you want to spend money, you can join a gym or buy expensive exercise equipment. But if you don't use either one, you'll save a lot of money by finding other choices. Many other ways are available that can be more fun and just as effective. Ride a bike or roller blade. If you're near a pool, swimming is the only exercise that works out every muscle in the body. A few years ago, I lived in a guarded gate community that had an Olympic size pool. During the summer, I walked up to the pool every day and swam 60 laps in the pool. I'd alternate laps, first 20 of the Australian crawl, then 20 of the sidestroke, and finally 20 of the breaststroke.

One day, as I was approaching the pool, I noticed a group of about twelve very much overweight women who had joined hands as they stood waist deep in the pool.

They began walking across the pool, heading for the other side. I found it incredibly annoying since it was a lap pool and that meant, since they were going widthwise, that I would not be able to do my laps. I also found it somewhat humorous since, if the entire idea was to lose weight, they had chosen the shortest distance, thereby insuring that they would not get the maximum benefit.

A lot of people exercise that way. It's called taking the easy way out. I don't necessarily subscribe to the "no pain, no gain" philosophy either. I've spent many hours exercising and had no pain at all. A brisk walk is painless and if you do it in a park, along the beach, or in a forest, it becomes magical.

Before I moved to Colorado, I used to start my day with a 40-minute exercise videotape. Behind my house was a wilderness park with huge hills bordering it and Green River at the base of the hills. I called it Lilliputian Land. At night, in the dark, the hills looked like Gulliver tied down by the little people. I used to picture him struggling with the ropes to escape. Lilliputian Land became my friend, my solace, and my sanctuary.

After my morning exercise tape, I took a 30-minute walk, the first 15 minutes of which were in my neighborhood as I headed up to the clubhouse. During that time, I did my daily meditations (more about this in the chapter on Spirituality). Once I arrived at the clubhouse, I headed straight for the children's playground. There I swung on the swings while I spoke with my inner child. Sometimes, I sang while I moved back and forth on the swing. It always put me in touch with that inner part of me that we often neglect. After a few minutes, I walked down to the path that went behind the houses and started eastward through the meadow and woods into Lilliputian Land. Rabbits scampered in front of me; birds sang noisy renditions of their favorite tunes.

Even when it was winter and dark when I left the house, I could have told you when the sun was about to make an appearance in front of me. The birds always started singing just before the sun poked its head over the horizon. If I were a blind man, I could have told you the sun was about to rise. Green River especially, as it followed the path, contributed to my morning serenade, splashing and gurgling its way to the sea.

In addition to the wonderful sounds, I was assailed with the fragrance of the meadow. I can't begin to define it but it smelled like a rare perfume, a musky, earthy fragrance that I've never been able to identify and never came across again. My physical senses tuned up like instruments in a fine orchestra. Soon my eyes also received a feast as I walked through meadow flowers, holly and ivy bushes and squash plants that grew like ground cover before me. As I rounded a curve, the cottonwoods and the oak trees met my eyes. I'd squint and hold my hand over my eyes to cut down on the glare of the rising sun as I looked up at the branches of the oak trees and saw mistletoe growing in thick clumps here and there.

Can you really call this 30-minute walk boring? We can't all live in Lilliputian Land but have you honestly looked around your neighborhood? Are there any parks? Do you live near the beach? A walk on the beach can become your own Lilliputian Land.

There are other ways to exercise that can be highly entertaining. After doing my exercise tape for a certain period of time, I realized I had memorized all the moves. Now I watch the evening news (or sometimes snippets of a movie on American Movie Classics) while I do my video. The time goes so fast that I hardly know I've done it.

How about yard work? What a great exercise! I once knew a lady that cleaned houses for a side job to earn money and found out that the greatest reward was she toned up her muscles and lost 20 pounds. I discovered that farmers in Nebraska lived longer than any other people. That puzzled me since I knew the diet of farmers included lots of high fat meats, bacon and eggs, and fatty dairy products. Then I realized that I don't know anyone that works as hard as farmers do. It makes up for their high-fat diet. For those who didn't know, if you have high cholesterol, you can change your ratio of good to bad cholesterol not just by increasing your fruits and vegetables but also by increasing your exercise. Sometimes, just doing the latter is sufficient to make a huge change in your risk for heart disease.

Even if you can't give up sweets or totally change your diet, a few changes here and there and some exercise will put your cholesterol and your waistline exactly where you want them. It's possible to lose up to fifteen pounds in three weeks just by giving up sweets and alcohol.

One day, I was visiting my dear friend Lois in Petersburg, the small town where I grew up. As we sat on the front porch, I watched an elderly lady across the street pruning her bushes. "Who's that?" I asked. "That's Lolly Shaeffer," Lois replied. "She's almost 100 years old and she prunes her bushes every day. It takes her a long time to get anything done because she's slow moving; but not only does she enjoy it, it's good exercise for someone her age."

"Probably the main reason she even reached her age," I said. I thought about Lolly a lot in the days to come.

When Tom and I lived on three and a quarter acres of wooded land in the Colorado Rockies, exercise was even more fun. I not only took my daily 45-minute walk, but I built a stump garden (you have no idea how much those stumps weigh — dragging them around was a great cardiovascular workout), dug a trench for a pebbled river bed with a beautiful log bridge across it, chopped wood, sawed down trees, shoveled piles of dirt to put under the foundation of our storage shed, and hauled wheelbarrows full of it to the road to build a berm.

One year, I dug a deep hole to plant a tiny lilac bush. Our friends made fun of my "stick bush" for the next year, claiming it would never see a single leaf. But I had the last laugh when my bush, after many private talks with it where I assured it that it would be the most beautiful lilac bush in the world, began sprouting green leaves and doubling its size almost overnight.

Look around you. Be creative. There are many ways to exercise that you probably haven't even thought of that you would enjoy. Try each one until you find the perfect physical activity. Keep in mind also that you are creating new behavior patterns and once set in place, they will become a part of your daily routine and you'll look forward to them. The added blessing of feeling euphoric and sleeping better will combine to make a healthier, happier you.

Have Regular Checkups and Practice Preventive Medicine

What a shame we don't realize how important this is till we get half way through our life! It's the rare person who begins practicing preventive medicine at a young age. We usually wait until a frightening symptom sends us to the doctor who in turn runs tests and then begins treating us with medication. From birth until we get somewhere in our forties, we exercise when we're in the mood, watch our diet and other health habits if we feel like it, smoke, drink to excess, and so on, never realizing that one day it's all going to catch up with us. Mostly, we just don't think about how we're setting up our bodies for destruction. Even with dental work, when we're younger, we may or may not have our teeth checked every six months. We pretty much brush on a regular basis but how many floss daily?

It's not too late to change those habits. Having an annual physical exam makes good sense. If it's a thorough exam, it'll include blood workup and a solid conversation with your doctor. He'll find out about your possible risk factors, family history etc. Keeping an eye on your weight, getting eye exams regularly, checking on cholesterol after a certain age, annual pap smears and mammograms for woman and prostate checkups for men make good sense. I had a bone density test done when I was 55. What a delight to find out that I had the bone density of a thirty-year old. But had the news not been so good, I would still be able to slow down the possibility of osteoporosis in my elder years by increasing my intake of calcium. This is something I've been doing for years and as you can see, it produced happy results.

If you eat healthy, drink plenty of water, and exercise regularly, starting at a young age, you'll find that by the time you get in your forties, you won't have the same health problems that others, who weren't following the same guidelines, will now be plagued with. I've seen so many people I love dearly who indulged themselves from the time they were grownups with cigarettes, excessive alcohol, no exercise, and bad diets, and are now plagued with cardiovascular problems, diabetes, obesity, and so on. Do you want to be one of them?

What's even sadder is when I see young people in their early twenties and younger that are already obese. Since almost everyone has a tendency to put weight on as they grow older, what chance do these people have? The time to begin preventive medicine is when you're young. Get started now.

Promote Good Grooming and Good Hygiene

This one should be fun. It's especially easy for us female of the species. We love shopping for clothes, getting our hair and nails done, taking bubble baths with scented candles, and so on. If men gloried in all the above, they'd be known as (an old-fashioned phrase) a "dandy" or effeminate. Not true. Women love a man who smells good, looks good, has neatly trimmed hair (and beard—I wish it were against the law for men to be clean shaven; a beard can cover a multitude of sins—weak chins for example). If he's wearing nicely fitted jeans and wearing crisp mountain logger plaid shirts, he'll cause some women to salivate. Some men have a great sense of style and don't need to be wearing an expensive three-piece suit to look sexy.

As we grow older, put on weight, and get bogged down by boring routines of married life, we tend to forget about looking good. Who cares, we've already got our man. Wasn't it Tammy Wynette that sang about the "other woman who knew a whole lot of tricks"? Don't take your mate for granted by letting yourself go, whether you're male or female. No one wants to be around someone with bad body odors or oily hair. Looking good means feeling good, about yourself and the world you live in. You may think your mate doesn't notice how you don't look as good as you did when you were younger but you can bet he (or she) will definitely stand at attention when they see that you're looking better and better as you lose weight, develop your own sense of style, and improve your grooming. The most important person you'll please is you.

Avoid Smoking, Alcohol, and Drugs.

Do we need to even go into this one!

Only someone who's severely dysfunctional or has a slow moving brain doesn't know the hazards of drugs. They don't show you a good time. They show you a slow and expensive death.

As for alcohol, there are pros and cons over this one. Italians tell you a couple glasses of wine a day are good for your heart. There may be some truth to that. I'm not an expert but having been married to two alcoholics (both deceased from it), I can tell you that with some people, two drinks only lead to two more and then two more. If a doctor told you that you can never drink again and your response was, "okay, no biggie," it's probably just fine to have a couple glasses of wine, but if you felt a sense of panic at the thought, the amount of your alcohol consumption may be something you want to take a closer look at.

Ah, the evils of smoking! Someone said once that the only best friend you'll ever have is a cigarette. As an ex-smoker, I agree and understand how tough this one is to give up. But would you have a best friend that led you down the path to possible lung cancer, almost certain heart problems, and absolutely certain premature aging and other health problems? Smoking is responsible for more deaths from coronary heart disease than for all types of cancer combined.

There are smoking cessation programs everywhere. Call the American Lung Association and they'll tell you where the nearest one is. Either that or check with your health care provider. While it may never be too late to quit—the decline in risk of death from coronary heart disease starts within the first year after quitting smoking and reduces the risk of death by up to 50%—there's no reason to postpone quitting today. Tomorrow may be too late.

Get Plenty of Sleep

It's been said that more than fifty percent of us suffer at one time or another from insomnia, especially the elderly. I had always thought that one of the blessings of growing older was that you'd now be able to get all the sleep you want. Not so. For a variety of reasons, the elderly suffer a great deal from this problem. Ironically enough, I read once that the single most important ingredient required in longevity is plenty of sleep. Over the years, it's plagued me to the point of desperation. Many a night, I have been unable to sleep for hours because of worrying about insomnia. If that doesn't make you crazy, nothing will. What to do? No one has a magic formula. Some things work and some only work for a short time. But I've been able to discover a few gems of wisdom in dealing with this problem that I'd like to share.

- Keep caffeine intake to a minimum.
- Use salt sparingly, if at all.
- A hot bath with a good book, soft music, and a lighted candle (white for serenity) has a calming effect before bedtime.
- Eat early in the evening and avoid large meals at that time if possible.
- Always retire at the same time.
- Avoid the use of prescription sleeping pills if at all possible. They only compound the problem as your body becomes dependent on them and can no longer fall asleep on its own.
- Establish a comforting and stabilizing ritual prior to bedtime, i.e. lay out clothes for the next day, brush

your teeth and bathe, set the clock, read something bland for a few minutes, before turning the light out.

- Avoid intense and worrisome phone calls before retiring, as well as any late-night dealings that may encourage stress (paying bills right before bed time will usually insure tossing and turning).

- Don't exercise to excess in the evening—a short walk perhaps to ease tensions. Keep in mind that daily exercise, especially the kind that elevates your heart rate, improves sleep.

- Make sure the room temperature is comfortable.

If you begin to toss and turn, get out of bed, and fix a glass of warm milk or non-caffeine herb tea. Since insomnia intensifies once you begin worrying about it, anything you can do to distract yourself, eliminates the problem (especially emptying the dishwasher).

I want to end this chapter by talking about the highest risk factor people can have in their physical health—stress. I've done a lot of thinking about people I've known who lived a long life and what they did different from those who died young. Most of the time, it had to do with unhealthy life styles, but I've also noticed a strong trend in the amount of stress people had in their lives and more importantly, how they reacted to situations that would normally have been stressful. The ones with the least stress lived longer. My Finnish grandfather lived to be 94 and was active and taking care of himself in his own home till almost the end. Only dizziness in the last year of his life prompted him to move into a nursing home. He ate sparingly (although he loved sweets) but not in a particularly nutritious manner, just pretty much what he wanted to. He never smoked or drank and wasn't all that physically active. His favorite recreations were fishing and hunting; both sports he did frequently. What he did have that was quite different from people I knew that died young was that he literally didn't do stress. My father died of a massive heart attack at age 71, but he was always angry. I never knew my grandfather to be angry. I only saw him upset once in his life and that was when he and I were out at his cabin in the woods and our car got stuck in the mud. That was before cell phones, the nearest neighbor was miles away, and grandpa was 92. I hiked to a nearby farmhouse and got help but that didn't keep grandpa from worrying. But as a general rule, he had a very dry sense of humor, was a plodding thinker and absolutely didn't let things upset him.

It's something to think about, how much stress contributes to health problems and an early demise. Telling yourself you just won't get angry or worry or get stressed no matter what happens won't work. Some of us by nature are worriers and high-stress people. What then? The amount of physical activity you do, your ability to avoid high stress people and high stress situations, a healthy diet and times of meditation, and relaxation can all offset even the most worrying, nervously intense person in the world.

Listen to Your Own Body as It Speaks to You

Tom and I moved to Arizona in 2003. During this fortuitous event, I had an interesting and unnerving experience. Our primary reason for moving there had to do with living at 9000 foot altitude in Bailey, Colorado and finding out how dangerous that altitude was for Tom's heart condition. During the second trip to transport, our many vehicles (we have eleven motorcycles, an ATV, a motor home, a '79 Ford pickup that Tom thinks is every man's dream, a Wrangler, and a Jeep Cherokee) as we were checking into a motel, I became disoriented and dizzy. I found it difficult to walk, and since we hadn't eaten in six hours, attributed it to low blood sugar. Within an hour of eating, the symptoms went away. Once we arrived in Cornville (don't laugh, that's the name of our town, but, located fifteen minutes south of Sedona, it's a place of not only spirituality, but magic), I scheduled a doctor's appointment. Agreeing with my diagnosis, he took blood tests. Before the results came back, we drove to the Los Angeles area to attend graduation ceremonies and parties for our grandchildren.

During that week, I had two more of what I was beginning to call "my episodes". In the first one, I was again disoriented and dizzy, but my speech was halting as well. In the second one, I was unable to talk. While my friends may have considered this a blessing, it frightened me. In both cases, I returned to normal within two hours. Once we returned to Arizona, I again spoke with my doctor. By now, I was convinced all of the symptoms were side effects from a medication I was taking. The doctor disagreed, thought I had either a brain tumor or had had a series of mini-strokes. He scheduled an MRI but the results were normal.

A week later, while Tom and I were on the third floor of our new home, I collapsed, unable to move, like a puppet whose strings had been cut and again was disoriented and unable to speak at all. Tom called an ambulance and I was taken to Emergency where a CAT Scan and more blood work were done. Within two hours, I began regaining both my ability to speak and my ability to move my body. I told the ER doctor that I thought it was side effects from medication. He disagreed and asked if I'd ever seen a psychiatrist. I wondered what that had to do with anything but admitted that several years earlier, I'd been in recovery for five years as a result of being raped by my Dad when I was thirteen. He told me I was suffering post traumatic stress and needed to see a psychiatrist. No amount of argument on my part swayed him to my way of thinking. He had a social worker spend two hours with me. At the end of our conversation, she agreed with me. I did not need to see a psychiatrist, had worked my way through recovery in an admirable manner, and in her opinion, it was a side effect of the drugs.

The next day, I emailed a physician friend of mine, giving him the details of both what had been happening to me and the medications I was taking. He responded by telling me that two different medications I was on had side-effects identical to what was happening. I immediately began cutting back on one of the medications. Within two days, I was in a neurologist's office. After listening to my story, studying the test results from the MRI, the blood workup and the CAT Scan, he agreed with my diagnosis. He took me off one of the medications and began weaning me off the other. I never had those symptoms again.

Listening to your own inner voices, especially regarding your health, is vital. My body knew all along what the problem was. Unfortunately, the medical profession didn't bother to check. Had I not believed in my own truth, I might not have been here. The next side effects waiting were a coma and death.

13 | Spiritual Dimension

What about that *soul* part of us? A life without any spiritual connection becomes empty and meaningless. If I had to list a few rules in the area of our spiritual dimension that promote good spiritual health, they would be as follows:

- Seek the guidance of a Higher Power on a daily basis.
- Spend time with spiritual reading, whether it be the Bible, the Koran, the Baghavagita, the *Lives of the Saints*, philosophical readings, Twelve Step literature, or anything of a spiritual nature.
- Set aside regular time for reflection, meditation, introspection, or just quiet time.
- Spend time in nature.
- Practice the "Three Acts of Kindness A Day" rule.
- Do a daily examination of conscience and ask your Higher Power for forgiveness.
- Work hard at understanding and accepting your own immortality; find a belief in the afterlife.

Let's break these rules down and find a way to make them work.

Seek the Guidance of a Higher Power on a Daily Basis

Not everyone believes in a Higher Power. That's okay. But everyone does believe that we came from somewhere, whether it's the stork or the hospital, or descended from apes, or the result of the hand of God. The wonderful thing about being a human is that we can choose our own beliefs.

Working the Twelve Steps, while I was in recovery, proved to be the best thing I ever did for myself. I met a lot of people who were uncomfortable with the first step: **I admitted I was powerless over others and that my life had become unmanageable.** For someone who had been raped as a child, the idea of being powerless was frightening. It took me more than two years to work my way through that first step. Step Two: **We came to believe that a power greater than ourselves could restore us to sanity.** Since I had always believed in a Higher Power, I had no problem with this. But many I met did. "I don't believe in God" was the comment I heard most often. And to them, a higher power meant God. When they finally understood that they could make a Higher Power anything they wished, they felt more in control and safer.

I am fortunate to have many friends, all different, all special. One of the finest is my friend Nancy. Nancy teaches English at a major university. She also does not believe in God. She belongs to a women's writers group (the same one I belonged to when I lived in California) that is strongly Christian. Almost all the women attend the same church, around which their lives and conversations center primarily. Quoting scriptures, entering their religious beliefs into dialogues, as well as having prayer circles during the meetings is a regular with them. Since the group was never initially started as a religious group, rather a women's writer's and support group, this presented a problem in Nancy's life. She was not judgmental about it, just uncomfortable at times. She is not only non-judgmental, she is caring, fiercely protective of Mother Nature; hearty rainstorms are one of her favorite things; and she cherishes her friends to the deepest level. How much more spiritual can you get than this?

It's not that I don't have a great deal of respect for other's religious paths; I've just never thought that organized religion was the only right one. Realizing I had the right to believe in whatever I wanted to, I returned to Catholicism on my terms after many years of being gone. I will no doubt be Catholic in my heart till I die and value those things that are good that I learned from the nuns and priests of my childhood. But I also value those truths I learned from studying other religions and others' spiritual paths.

The idea of finding a Higher Power is to take your problems off your own shoulders and place them elsewhere, anywhere—in the woods, in the mountains, near the ocean, in a box under your bed—whatever you are comfortable with. Let them go. Once you do that, there's a lightening of the heart. In seeking the guidance of a Higher Power on a daily basis, you are only releasing yourself from the problems and 'pretending', if you wish, that someone else will help you handle them. You don't need a huge imagination to make this happen. Who among us has never imagined winning the lottery? If you can do that, you can imagine someone or something that's waiting in the shadows to bear your burdens for you. Keep 'pretending' and it will soon feel real.

Spend Time Reading Something of a Spiritual Nature

Boring you say. I know, I know. The only reading you like is Robert Ludlum or Stephen King. Spiritual reading is just not entertaining. This may not be true. Start by going through several choices in your library. By spiritual reading I mean anything that pertains to the development of the soul. That could encompass not only manuscripts of a religious nature but books about integrity, about changing unhealthy behavior patterns. It doesn't have to be a book written by someone from an organized religion or the Bible (although I've always been impressed with Abraham Lincoln saying that all the wisdom he learned came from that book). It's my belief that even an atheist could write a deeply spiritual book. At least one is bound to catch your attention, if you find nothing in the philosophical or the theological section look on the self-help shelves. Even the great classics sometimes fall into the category of spiritual reading. It is hard to read Chaucer's *Canterbury Tales*, without finding out something meaningful about life. If I owned only one book, it would be a thin volume that takes only an hour to read—*As A Man Thinketh* by James Allen. It is food for the soul.

Discipline yourself to read one page a night from whatever book you choose. You can do that. The second week, read two pages a night. If by then you find nothing impressive or helpful in what you're reading, go back to the library and locate another book. I guarantee that in no time something will plant a seed of awareness and the willingness to turn your life around.

Set Aside Time for Reflection, Meditation, Introspection

This was a hard one for me. I'm a hyperactive person who always has to have several projects going at one time. I'm organized and goal-oriented, making endless to-do lists. Nothing pleases me more than to rush from one activity to another and cross out at the end of the day all my accomplishments. Then I met Tom. What he likes to do most is power lounge. He's quite good at it and convinced me that power lounging relaxed me and made it easier for me to get a good night's sleep.

While living in Colorado, our happiest moments were sitting on our decks. As I mentioned previously, before moving to Arizona, we lived on three and a quarter acres in the Colorado Rockies; land filled with pine trees and forested ground cover, complete with stumps, fallen logs, branches, and pine needles. Near the front deck, we had two feeders, one for hummingbirds hanging on a tree branch and a bird feeder attached to a galvanized pipe mounted to the deck. The view in front of us was a stack of neatly chopped wood wedged between two trees, a horse-drawn plow from Tom's father's farm where he grew up, a randomly stacked pile of wood, another bird bath, a bird feeder on a pole, a salt lick, and a large plastic tub of water for our critters to drink from.

We spent happy hours watching our low maintenance pets, squirrels, chipmunks, chickadees, hummingbirds, woodpeckers, a host of other birds, and often a small herd of deer or elk that leisurely wandered across our land. One time, this included a large black bear who was lopping across our wooded acreage. We've watched the deer play "ring around the rosy" through the pine trees and named our favorite female deer Jane Doe and her mate Buck Rogers. We were especially fond of three chipmunks we've named Winkin, Blinkin, and Nod. The smell of pine trees, the song of the chickadees, and the wind in the pines, and especially the show that birds and squirrel put on for us brought hours of joy and serenity. We watched hummingbirds fight over perches, gray squirrels make love, and chipmunks play hide and seek in our woodpile. Who needs television? Moving to Arizona made no difference in our joy of the land; only now it's desert and mountains, sunsets and awesome cloud arrangements, rattle snakes, lizards, and javalinas (small, boar-like herbivores).

During the morning walk I used to take, I had a daily meditation. It included my list of things to thank my creator for, my "turning over to God" requests for various friends and family, my own goal setting in the area of the six dimensions as well as other goals and repeating the Serenity Prayer, The Twelve Steps, The Desiderata, St. Francis of Assisi's prayer, and the Ten Promises. All of this reinforced healthy mental attitudes and an almost euphoric air of positive thinking. It empowered me to handle challenges I might have during the day. Between the exercise and the meditation, not only did I sleep deeply every night, but also I began most days with a perfect attitude that continued throughout the day.

Quiet time is your mind's way of recharging batteries. We all lead busy lives and tell ourselves that one day we're going to slow down, but that day never comes. Force yourself (I think I should have titled this book, *Force Yourself* to set aside a few minutes a day to do nothing.

A word about introspection. Despite being a firm believer in Aristotle's famous phrase 'An unexamined life is not worth living,' I heard a comment on an educational tape the other day that proved to be thought provoking. The professor giving the lecture (which was about philosophy) mentioned Aristotle's comment and added one of his own. "Most suicides are caused by too much introspection." First of all, I disagreed; but after giving it some thought, I realized that here again one must keep balance in mind. It's great to examine your own life but when you find yourself obsessing needlessly and unproductively on something problematical in your life, it could lead to a multitude of dark thoughts that do nothing but add to the problem.

A while back, there was a lot of publicity about a man who took his beloved two-year-old son into the woods with him. He planned on doing some hunting and the son fell asleep in the car before he arrived at his destination. He decided that rather than awaken his young son, he'd let him sleep and go off and do some hunting by himself. The son woke up some time after his father left, wandered off into the woods, and was found dead five days later. The father was charged with child neglect and sentenced to a month in jail. The day before his sentence began, he killed himself. One can only imagine the dark thoughts that spiraled around in this poor man's mind. Many a mother, not wanting to awaken their sleeping child, has left them in the car, albeit keeping an eye on them from the house. It is thinking about this particular case that made me realize the professor was correct. I knew there were many times when I had dwelled on something long past when I needed to and found myself feeding fears and building up what might otherwise be a problem I could learn to either resolve or live with.

Spend Time in Nature

Nature has a way of soothing the soul. If you are in the midst of a forest, on the shore of an ocean, at the top of a mountain, or perhaps just standing in a cornfield, you are in touch with that soul part of you. I wrote a volume of poems once called *Things of God and Things of Man*. To me, anything that had to do with nature, plants, flowers, trees, mountains, bodies of water, and so on, were things of God. Anything man produced—houses, furniture, cars, boats, and even activities such as parties etc.— were things of man.

We all obviously need things of man in our life. We need things of God as well. There are many things that, to me, are things of God: a child's shy smile, the faces of the elderly, the look on a deer's face when he's watching me watch him, a chipmunk scampering on our wood pile, then stopping to nuzzle his mate, clouds drifting and making lovely patterns against a sky of deepest blue, a storm with wild bolts of lightning and crashes of thunder that sound as if the roof is caving in, snow-flakes on my tongue, hail on the roof, a sunrise or a sunset, the smell of pine trees in the woods, especially after a rain, the smell of fresh mown grass, the music of Chopin or Tchaikovsky or Beethoven, Joyce Kilmer's poem about trees, and on and on and on. I'm very blessed. I find that the simplest things bring me joy. And when I have joy, I have peace and what's more important, I have spiritual growth.

Practice Three Acts of Kindness A Day

I stumbled on this little gem by accident. When I was still working in an office, one day I noticed how many potlucks, collections for birthdays, new babies, and prospective weddings there were, to say nothing of the community walk-a-thons etc. I felt incredibly guilty. I almost never brought anything to a potluck, preferring to spend my lunchtime in solitude, reading a book, since that's how I recharged my battery. I rarely put anything in a collection. Since they asked for money almost weekly and with a 20-member family, I was already spending a lot on other people ("charity begins at home," my mother always said). And as for community Walk-A-Thons, with an hour and a half commute each way (in bad weather, 2 to 3 hrs each way) by the time I left work, it was all

I could do to get out of town and up the mountain before it grew dark. And the idea of driving back into town on a weekend exhausted me.

So I made my excuses while feeling like I needed to go to confession and then say at least five rosaries. The one that guilted me the most was the Diabetes Walk-A-Thon. I had a beloved granddaughter with diabetes. Why couldn't I at least join that? I spent several days berating myself. Then, one day, entirely by accident, I went out of my way to do something special for a co-worker. She was extremely grateful. I thought about that. What if I could do the minimum of one act of kindness a day for someone else? What if I could do a minimum of three acts of kindness a day? I thought about how most people do little things for others throughout their day and never give it a thought. It's all part of living in a community. But what if I made sure that all my acts of kindness were things that I wouldn't normally do? Better yet, what if I did them anonymously?

I began my project. Within days, I noticed that I was looking for acts of kindness that would especially enhance a person's day. I overheard a co-worker say she had high blood pressure and what a pain it was to have to go to the doctor all the time to get it tested. I remembered that Tom and I owned three blood pressure machines. What did we need with three? I put an extra one on her desk. Another co-worker shared with me that the Sales Agent she worked for treated her like a lackey, never saying thank you, always chastising her for not doing good enough. I tried to imagine what my day would be like if I had a superior like that. My boss was kind and thoughtful. Then one day, her Sales Agent noticed a post it on the computer of her back up support person saying she was at an interview. She became alarmed. Somewhat teasingly I responded that yes, Jeanne was at an interview. "Is she looking for another job?" The Sales Agent's alarm grew.

"Well, actually," I responded, "She's hoping to find one where she gets treated like a queen. She's such a wonderful lady that she deserves to be treated like a queen." The Sales Agent could only stare at me with consternation. I could almost hear the wheels in her head spinning. "Are you pulling my chain?" she asked. "Maybe," I answered, as I walked back to my desk. An immediate change began to happen in the relationship between the Sales Agent and Jeanne.

So you see, opportunities exist everywhere to make someone's day better. You might not work in three every day but you can certainly average three a day. Can you imagine what kind of world we would have if everyone practiced three acts of kindness a day? Get started. You'll find the main benefit coming in the increase in your own sense of well-being.

Do a Daily Examination Of Conscience

One of the practices I learned growing up in the Catholic Church was the Examination of Conscience. Established to help one prepare for confession, it became a ritual that I practice to this day. Itemizing your sins and shortcomings is a good way to be aware that you are human and have a few "growth of the soul" items that need taking care of. I have my own one-on-one conversations with God where I list my shortcomings and my willingness to eliminate them. While it doesn't necessarily help me to become the more perfect person I'd like to be, it does keep these faults in my line of vision. If the most I learn from this is to apologize to someone I've hurt and to try to do better, it's a healthy behavior pattern. Most importantly, it helps me understand human frailties, especially my own.

Understand and Accept Your Own Immortality

If there's any one subject I have contemplated more than any other, it's whether or not there is an afterlife. After much reading, discussion, meditating, and asking questions, I've come to the conclusion that there is. Most people believe there is something after death. We just disagree on exactly what that is. Children are told it means going to heaven and heaven is often portrayed as white clouds, angels with wings playing harps, St. Peter at the pearly gates and, most importantly, a father-like figure with a long white beard and a wise look—who is God. Exactly what happens after we get there is also subject to debate and even those who have an idea are fuzzy about what that idea is.

Consider the *Twilight Zone* episode called "A Nice Place to Visit" where the main character (a crook) died. When he came to, he had a guide named Pip (played by the late Sebastian Cabot) who escorted him through his new life. Here he could have whatever he wanted, whenever he wanted it and as often as he wanted. He was ecstatic. He'd lived a very evil life and if he'd been asked before he died whether he was going to heaven or hell, there would have been no doubt where he would wind up. But here he was with the fulfillment of his slightest wish at his command; obviously he'd gone to heaven. He proceeded to take full advantage of this bountiful place. He had the company of beautiful, shapely women; he ate the most delicious food he could ever imagine; he listened to mind blowing music, whatever his mood chose; he had the most beautiful home and the most expensive cars he'd ever dreamed of. All he had to do was snap his fingers and it was his. Even when he gambled, he always won, won, won. He couldn't believe his good fortune and day after day, week after week indulged himself in everything and anything he wanted.

After several months of this, he grew bored. One day while gambling and again winning by the millions, he turned to Pip and said. "I'm tired of this. I want to lose for a change." He waited for this to happen. But it didn't. He kept on winning. Now very agitated, he again insisted he didn't want to win and not only that, he didn't want gourmet meals; he wanted a slightly burned hamburger. And another thing, he wanted a homely woman who was flat-chested. (I'm paraphrasing here). Burl Ives kept shaking his head with a secretive and knowing smile. The man went into a rage, demanding over and over that he didn't want anything his heart desired. It was making him nuts. It soon dawned on him that he wasn't in heaven. He was in hell.

It's an interesting concept of getting what you always wanted. I, for one, have always found this picture of heaven with its angels and harps and clouds and especially the old man with the flowing white beard a bit silly. And I think most people, once they grow up, would agree. But what do you replace it with?

I want to start with a theory I have. I think we all create the time of our own deaths. Not consciously of course, although some people do that as well. Those who smoke, who are overweight, who don't exercise, who take chances in racing or mountain climbing or other dangerous pursuits are unwittingly saying that it's okay with them to cut down their chances of a long and healthy life. I think often of the days before I went into recovery and how I lived a life of despair, often trying to take my own life and angry when I failed. My sense of humor prompts me at times to ask my higher power to please disregard previous instructions. Had I succeeded, one could say in all honesty that I created the time of my own death.

But what about the child who dies of cancer, the woman trapped in a fire, the innocents who are killed in automobile accidents that are the fault of another? How could they possibly have created the time of their own death?

I propose that there is another dimension to our psyche, one I will call the 'other world' dimension. In this dimension, the soul reigns supreme. The soul that is all-knowing and all-seeing and all-powerful and is—by the definition of all religions —eternal, knows what it needs to achieve its own growth. Perhaps it needs to drop its current body in order to link with another and achieve the next stage in its development. This theory only works if one believes in reincarnation. If you're not one, it couldn't hurt to at least check it out. Find a book on reincarnation, read it, think about it, and make your own decision. If you still don't believe it's a reality, there's always the possibility that some souls are only meant to spend a short time as a human before they are able to achieve permanent spiritual bliss.

It is difficult for most humans to believe that one day they will be here and the next day—*poof*— gone. It makes no sense. Once we understand and believe that humans have choices, it is only one step further to comprehend that the ultimate choice of all, deciding how and when we will drop our body, even if it's done on an unconscious level, is much more in our hands than we realize.

Even plants, trees, and flowers are not here one day and gone the next. Under the earth, there is always a seed that comes back in the spring or a blossom that reappears or another tree that grows in place of the old one, from a tiny acorn perhaps. Why would humans, who are so much more advanced on the biological scale, just disappear? It's absolutely absurd to think that one day we won't exist. Nature really does abhor a vacuum. It, meaning even humans, may change form, but will never disappear.

I have often heard of people who die in the very way they have spent most of their life fearing. That fear was born of an unconscious knowledge. The soul part knew something that the body part wouldn't accept as truth. Natalie Wood, for one, was terrified of dark water. I have often heard people say, "I'm not going to live to a ripe old age. I'll, no doubt, die young". I hope they're not surprised when that happens. Often your body takes statements such as this to be an instruction that must be followed.

Grant Lewi, a famous astrologer from the thirties and forties kept an accurate calendar of all his appointments and on a month-to-month basis, he had his workdays filled with people's names that had consultations scheduled with him. After he died, it was discovered that his calendar for the month in which he died had appointments up until the day before his death and none thereafter. He hadn't been planning on retiring or taking a vacation. He just knew that on that day he would drop his body.

There are countless stories of people who planned the last few days of their lives as if they knew they had a limited time left. My sister Jeanne, whose story I have referenced in this manuscript earlier, knew that her own death was approaching. She was unafraid and found the idea of death to be the last great adventure.

But for most humans, the thought of death is terrifying, especially knowing we can't contact those we left behind nor can they contact us. This may or may not be true. I, for one, have had more than one conversation with someone from the other side. It just doesn't happen very often and for reasons I haven't yet figured out (but intend to someday) happens only to a select few.

For those who die in agony—and when you think of the battlefields, the fires, and the accidents, there are many—it is much worse. People who have lived a life of misery may welcome leaving it, whether they believe in the afterlife or not. And who can blame them? For the majority of people who have lived on planet earth, life has not been a pleasant experience. Many are poverty-stricken, starving, have traumatizing events happen to them, find little joy, and just eking out a living is more than they can handle.

I recently finished listening to a 48 lecture series on the *History of the Civil War*. The anguish that most Americans lived through during that four-year period is almost unbelievable. More men were killed in that war than in all the other combined United States wars ever fought. The number of men who had limbs amputated, sometimes not just an arm but an arm and a leg, at times without any painkillers, is staggering. When you add the number of families that watched their homes and livelihood burn to the ground, the brothers who fought against brothers, the shear starvation and disease that plagued the nation, especially the south, it is almost too sad to contemplate.

Why? Why? Why? There absolutely has to be a reason why mankind has had to go through so much grief and anguish. It can't just be a random crapshoot. Unfortunately, we humans have a difficult time seeing the big picture. While it may be true that we are all as a grain of sand on the beach, it is also true that all together, we are a lovely, sandy beach. We must one day, drop our bodies; we must, at one time or another, suffer adversity. Why again? It has been said that more opportunities to forge one's character exist during war times than at any other time. When I first heard that, I was dismayed and not sure I believed it. But upon giving it more thought, I realized (gulp) much truth dwelled in those words.

Think about courage. What a great character for the soul to develop. In being thrown in the midst of a war, you may or may not achieve this. It's your call. What about patience, persistence, endurance, and loyalty to one's fellow man? What about the compassion one gains when seeing man's inhumanity to man? The very quality of intestinal fortitude—the ability to endure whatever comes your way—can best be developed during war-time. Sad, you say? Of course, it's sad. And wouldn't it be wonderful if everything were just perfect and there were no bad times? What if there were no Four Horsemen of the Apocalypse; no one had to die or to ever suffer.

Why then, we'd be just like the man who thought he had wound up in heaven after he died, only to find out it was hell. We'd have nothing to compare the good times with if all were only good. That may sound trite, but sometimes the joys in life are so much sweeter when one has gone through a period of adversity. This is life, the good along with the bad.

And death is also a part of life. But it is not the ending. It is rather a beginning. What does it look like? No one knows, not for sure. You're free to pick you own scenario. For me, there will be people I love deeply who have already dropped their bodies that I'll be able to see again. Just dropping my own body, knowing I'll be free from disease, from exhaustion, from insomnia, from a myriad of unpleasant things associated with the body sounds like heaven to me, at least if the ending comes when I'm quite elderly, have accomplished all I want to and especially can take my awareness with me.

I've often thought about all those rooms in my mind that contain bad memories, wishing that a snap of my fingers would remove them. It's my belief that once you drop your body, those memories will lose their sting. We'll have other senses, other awareness capabilities. So perhaps one will be able to view the events in their life dispassionately, objectively, without emotional pain. This is what I choose to believe. You can choose whatever you like. The important thing is to have a belief system in place.

When I was a child, the Catholic religion taught me about heaven, hell, limbo, and purgatory. Heaven was vague, limbo was even more so, but they were quite definite about hell and purgatory. The nuns would tell us to hold our hand over a flame if we wanted to see what waited if we were bad. Purgatory was going to hurt as well but at least it was temporary. In fact, if you paid enough money or said enough prayers, you could get indulgences to wipe out your time in purgatory. I used to sit as a child and add up how much time I'd have to serve in purgatory. Thinking bad thoughts about my sister, the one I didn't get along with, was good for at least a year. I knew that. Not saying my morning prayers was probably going to insure I'd have to spend an additional six months feeling the flames of purgatory. And once I learned about masturbation, I figured I was doomed. It was all pretty scary.

The fact that the church gave me a list of rules for what was wrong and right and didn't allow me to decide for myself made it even scarier. I wondered why there was a commandment to honor thy father and thy mother but none to honor thy children. Why could a parent do great harm to their child physically, emotionally, and/or mentally (sometimes even sexually), and it wasn't a sin? On the other hand, a child who "talked back" to their parents was sure to spend a great deal of extra time in purgatory. The one I really had a tough time with was "coveting thy neighbor's wife". First of all, I had no idea what coveting meant but I wondered why there was no commandment for coveting thy neighbor's husband. During my severely dysfunctional years, I used to crack jokes about how that must be okay. I found the entire list of rules and regulations confusing and unfair.

When I was in my teens, the nuns at St. John the Baptist school announced there was a book in the library about Cain and Abel that we were not allowed to read. If we did so, it would be a mortal sin. For those of you who are not Catholic, a mortal sin not confessed and forgiven before you die means that you will go straight to hell. A mortal sin was often described as adultery, fornication (as a naïve teenager I wasn't sure what those two were), murder, missing mass (I was also never quite sure why that was lumped in with murder and adultery), and/or stealing something major. A venial sin, on the other hand, which was usually described as a lie, an unpleasantness to someone else, or stealing something minor, would earn you time in purgatory even if it was confessed.

This matter of the offensive book got in my head and within hours, I had snuck in to the library, confiscated the said book (adding stealing to my list of sins—but if I was going to hell because of a mortal sin, it was in for a penny in for a pound) and devoured it. I learned two things. It was a boring book and if they thought it was a mortal sin to read it, why did they tell us about it in the first place, thereby putting temptation in our path. Not only that, if it was so offensive why did they even have it?

To me, the Catholic religion was a great breeding ground to figure out some of the answers to life. Without the absurdity of "truths", the nuns taught me I would never have questioned anything. My spiritual growth would have halted at the age of twelve. It should continue until you drop your body. Not only does it make life more rewarding, it brings a sense of peace and orderliness as well as a sense of purpose, to the whole idea of existence.

The opportunity for spiritual growth is everywhere. Several years ago, I took a writing class from a Pulitzer Prize winner. At one of the sessions, he wanted each of us to share a poem we had written. He began with one he had written entitled "All the Places My Tongue has Been." One doesn't need an x-rated mind to picture what the poem was about. Despite having an earthy sense of humor, I was embarrassed. When it came time to share mine, I read a poem I'd written called "Courage". After finishing, I noticed there was an uncomfortable silence. In looking around the table, I realized each of the potential authors had looks of dismay on their faces. One of the gals gave me a condescending look, followed by a comment dripping with sarcasm, "noble sentiments, no doubt". It was obvious the rest of the group were of the same opinion. My first response was to feel humiliated, but when driving home that night, I decided that

Noble Sentiments would be a wonderful title to a volume of poems I was writing, all of them about "noble sentiments."

I'm very grateful to the young lady and choose to believe that words written about the finer things in life, meaning words of wisdom and higher values, far surpass words about what I might possibly do with my tongue.

One night, I had a dream. It was so vivid that I felt like I wasn't in my body. I was in someone else's. I was living in a small village, a young girl, barefoot and wearing a long robe. My emotions were heavy, a life so far filled with trauma and anger. The hopelessness and the dark pictures in my head seemed to weigh more than I could bear. I started to walk through the village, feeling the sand beneath my feet as it wriggled through my toes, feeling the warmth of the sun as it gently stroked my shoulders, even though I didn't feel either one as a pleasure. Soon I came to the village well.

A young man, also dressed in a long robe, was taking water from it. He saw the sadness in my eyes and asked me what was wrong. Not used to sharing with strangers, I nevertheless began pouring my heaviness out. He listened intently, a kind look on his face. His eyes were so gentle that somehow just looking at them lightened my load. Then he began speaking. He talked about forgiveness and peace and little by little, gently guided me into seeing the other side of my dark picture. I can't recall his words, only the tone of voice, so low I had to cock my head to listen. He painted a picture with his words, one of a world filled with joy. He pointed out the goodness in human nature and spoke of man's frailties as if they were sometimes a sad thing, but only human.

The more he spoke, the lighter became my heart. I felt myself pull away from the anger and the hopelessness of life. I don't know how long he spoke but as time went on, the sky seemed a deeper blue, the clouds frothy things to attach oneself to and fly away on. The birdsong, so melodious it was like listening to a symphony, brought the beginning of rapture to my aching heart. He smiled as he saw the anger leaving me and reached out to touch me, his fingers so light they felt like feathers.

Then he reached into his robe and took a towel out. He put the towel to his face and patted his brow and his cheeks, holding the cloth to his face for a moment. After pulling it away, he handed it to me. I looked down at it and saw the print of his face on the towel. Below his face were drops of red, the color of blood. I gazed up at him, a startled look in my eyes. Again, he had a gentle smile, the depth of blue in his eyes almost matching the blue of the sky.

"What is this?" I said in a low voice. "Is it blood?"

He looked up at the sky as if something were written there that he was trying to read, then looked at me again. "There will be more to come," was his reply. "It will be shed so that all men will see the joy of life and know the peace that is buried in their heart is theirs for the asking." Then he turned and walked away.

I awoke with a start, the memory of my dream still vivid in my mind as I remembered the other side of life that he had described and it seemed truly as if the joy he had spoken of were mine for the asking. I wondered if I had been that young girl 2000 years ago, or was it a dream.

I tell you this story to show you that life is not what it seems to those of us trudging through it in hopes of one day a miracle happening and we might see the "other side". One doesn't have to be a Christian to feel joy. One only has to develop the spiritual side of our nature; then reach for the rapture.

I want to share another story that, although it may sound heart-wrenching, is one that I cherish. In 1987, a man I was engaged to was dying of cancer. He was the finest thing that had ever happened to me and treated me as if I were the most cherished thing he'd ever known. He had become convinced that something traumatic had happened to me when I was a child for he couldn't understand how someone as wonderful as he thought

I was would wind up with so many abusive men. As a result, he began an investigation that caused me to push him away by doing things I will regret till I die. My unconscious fear that he was getting too close to something I was terrified of facing was the reason for my attempts to distance myself from him.

At the pronouncement of lung cancer, Chuck became terrified. I knew the best thing I could do to repay him for his kindness to me was to prepare him for his own death. I did just that, telling him what my belief system contained, encouraging him to develop his own. I was strongly convinced that he was only going to drop his body and enter another world, a world of peace and joy. I wanted him to believe that too. I was absolutely certain that he would be able in some way to let me know he was on the other side and had retained his awareness. In his less frightening moments, he assured me he would.

We had purchased a lovely two-story home with an upstairs master bedroom that had a floor-to-ceiling window overlooking a wilderness park (Lilliputian Land). Having grown up in the Midwest, I loved the sound of crickets and found them soothing. As a habitual insomniac, any solution to my problem was gratifying. This was one of them, for within minutes after opening the window and listening to them, I would fall asleep.

Chuck, who had been a city boy all his life, found this quality of mine endearing and periodically teased me about it, saying I was just a country girl at heart.

Once he asked me, from his hospital bed, that if, after he died, he found a way to let me know that he was okay, did I want him to do that? Of course, I did

On the day of his funeral, having gotten almost no sleep for weeks during the final agonizing days of his illness, I was in a state of severe exhaustion. The insomnia that plagued me so often ruled my life during that time. My right arm had developed a violent tremble that exhausted me. Chuck had assured me in the final hours that I had prepared him well for death and that he no longer minded dying. He only minded leaving me. It only made my anguish deeper.

After the final guest had departed from our home, I told my daughter and her husband, who were spending the night downstairs on my sleeper sofa, that I was going to bed. I almost crawled up the stairs, climbed into bed, and remembered no more until the unpleasant ringing of the phone twelve hours later interrupted my deep slumber. It was my daughter.

"Mom, are you okay?"

'Tammie, what are you doing calling me! I thought you were downstairs, sleeping."

"I was, Mom, but we woke up this morning and went home. Something happened last night that I need to tell you."

"What?"

"I was sound asleep when all of a sudden I was awakened by a white light. The room was filled with it and when I looked over at the drapes, I saw that they were billowing even though the patio door was shut. I had the strong and frightening feeling that someone was in the room, standing next to me. And the scariest thing was the room was filled with the sound of crickets. It was overwhelming. I plugged my ears and all of a sudden, the white light and the cricket noise and the presence I'd felt moved into the living room and headed up the stairs. I jumped up and hurried after it as I was frightened for you. It came to your bedroom door and went through it. I looked underneath at the crack and saw that your room was filled with the white light. The presence and the cricket noise had gone in too. I was so terrified I ran back downstairs and jumped into bed, holding on to Mark for dear life. Do you have any idea what it means Mom?"

After hanging up the phone, I took a walk in Lilliputian Land, my mind in deepest thought. I climbed a favorite cottonwood tree, sat on its branches as I watched Green River flow by and thought of the final words to Chuck's favorite psalm: "The Greatest of These is Love."

14 | Social Dimension

On the surface, one would think that paying high regard to our social dimension is not really of any prime importance. But take a second look. We spend our entire life interacting with others, our family, our friends, our co-workers, and the man on the street. Without certain social skills, our life would be lacking in an area that needs addressing on a daily basis. If I had had to list five rules in the area of our social dimension that promote good social health, they would be as follows:

- Develop excellent listening skills; this means not only hearing, but also responding to what you hear.
- Avoid toxic people.
- Be gracious and kind on a regular basis.
- Avoid hasty judgments and self-absorption; instead develop strong character and personal integrity.
- Develop a sense of humor.

Let's break these rules down and find a way to make them work.

Developing Excellent Listening Skills

Knowing that a great listener is worth their weight in gold and that a motor mouth is not only rude but hogs the conversation can cause me to feel dismay when I fail in this area. This has encouraged me to think before I speak. I also realized that you learn a lot more by listening and that most people are not really interested in hearing your voice. In my attempt through the years to become a better listener, I often thought of how much wisdom I was missing by expounding on my own opinions rather than listening to others. I already knew what I was thinking so why not see what others had to say.

I also discovered that those who were the best listeners had a sense of humility about them. Humility is not a bad word. Webster defines it as "not proud or "haughty", "not arrogant". To look at the flip side of this coin, arrogance on the other hand means exaggerating or disposed to exaggerating one's own worth or importance in an overbearing manner. There is a lot of personal power in humility and none in arrogance. Which one of these two would you like to be?

Many people wondered what the Duke of Windsor saw in Wallis Simpson. What was there about this almost homely woman who was already middle-aged that so captured the heart of a king that he gave up his throne for her. It has been said that she was a consummate listener, hanging on his every word. She also never told him what he wanted to hear but rather spoke her own truth. For a man who had never really been listened to and had been surrounded by yes-men all his life, this must have been enchanting. It's no wonder he fell so deeply in love with her.

I have a few more words about being a good listener that may not seem pertinent. I used to have a sign hanging in my bathroom that proclaimed, "Silence is the only successful substitute for brains." There are times when these words carry a lot of wisdom. Another popular saying that is in the same league with this one is "Speak softly and carry a big stick". People who come from a place of strong self-esteem and confidence have no need to bluster and bellow. In fact, the quieter the tone of your voice, the more it compels the listener to pay attention. Use fewer words when you do speak and back them up with the courage of your own convictions. Remember that less is more.

Avoid Toxic People

How does one define toxic people? Most of us know instinctively who they are but are reluctant to define them as such. That isn't Christian. I've found that a great many "Christian" people have no clue what Christ's teachings were really all about. There are many clues to the discovery of whether or not someone is a healthy person to have in your life. Do they put you down a lot? Do they always dump their problems on you without listening to yours? Do they say one thing and do another? Do you see them practicing integrity on a daily basis or are they untrustworthy? The person who repeats confidences to you that others have given them is also going to repeat your confidences. The person who does not carry their own weight in a project but instead finds ways to manipulate you into doing it by yourself is a toxic person. Anyone who does not respect your opinions but instead tries to browbeat you into theirs is not a healthy person to be around.

I used to work with a woman who spoke a lot about the teachings of Christ. While having a conversation with her one day, she began bad mouthing a woman in the department. I was surprised since she was usually so nice to the woman's face. She mentioned that the woman read tarot cards and visited psychics, going on and on about how terrible that was. I listened to what she had to say and then mentioned that I had studied Astrology for years and found that it had merit. I also mentioned that the three Wise Men that had visited Jesus at his birth were actually Astrologers. A shocked look came on her face and with a tight lip she said, "How can you believe in something so evil?" When I asked her what was evil about it, she began sputtering quotes from the Bible; then, confused about her own words, she stormed off with a parting shot, "I'll pray for you." My response, "good, I can use a few extra prayers," didn't endear me to her.

I decided the last thing I needed was someone who attempted to devalue me for my own belief system. I didn't devalue her for hers. Within a few short weeks, I noticed that she spent the majority of her day gathering gossip from one person and trotting around the office sharing it with others while putting in many hours of overtime doing nothing, giving her a nice fat pay check each week. I share this with you not out of a sense of judgment but a sense of observation. She has her ways and I have mine. The difference is that, since I found her to be toxic, I chose to not be in her space. When someone violates your sense of trust, one is better off leaving them to their own devices and finding someone that can add value to your life. If someone is not contributing things of value to your life, but instead filled with negative comments and put downs, they are toxic. Here again, listening is a valuable tool in discovering the difference between another's healthy or unhealthy behavior. Pay attention and act accordingly.

Be Gracious and Kind on a Regular Basis

If you watch the people that have the most friends, the ones who others gravitate to, you'll no doubt discover that they are gracious and kind. I made a list of the people I most loved and admired, the ones that had made the biggest difference in my life. I then made a list of the qualities they had that I loved the most, the ones I would like to emulate. All of them had one thing in common. They were consistently gracious and kind.

Who can help but want to be around people who have these qualities? The more you utilize them, the more they will become a part of your daily life. Always keep in mind that the more virtuous qualities you foster in yourself, the better your life will go and the straighter will be your path in life.

When you have done wrong, apologize. Oh I couldn't do that, you say. Why not? It doesn't weaken you, rather it makes you stronger. Nothing is more disarming than frankness and having the courage to say you made a mistake and you're sorry has not only a cleansing property but will cause those around you to respond with admiration and wish they too had the courage to be honest when it is required. Besides, it has the added benefit of making you aware of your own shortcomings and setting you on the road to correcting them. We all have shortcomings. So what? Work on them. Life will be more rewarding once you do.

I decided one day to list the twelve qualities I would most like to have. It was an interesting list and consisted of:

- Humility
- Great listener
- Courageous
- Gracious
- Compassionate
- Non-judgmental
- Emotionally controlled when needed and passionate about what mattered most
- Disciplined
- Devoted to those you love
- Purposeful in life
- Strong sense of personal integrity
- Dedicated to the pursuit of knowledge

If you work towards developing these qualities, you'll not only feel better about yourself, which builds self-esteem, but others will feel better about you.

Avoid Hasty Judgments and Self-Absorption

This one has always been a toughie for me. I'm so blasted opinionated and (as all opinionated people do) think mine are correct, much to the occasional dismay of those who have to listen to me expound on my judgments. It's been a real challenge to find ways to fix this problem. I have a sister-in-law that I'm not crazy about (doesn't everyone have someone like that in their lives?) who once made a comment about me (repeated to me by another sister-in-law I cared a great deal for—now there's something to wonder about) that was hurtful. Her comment? "A little of Margie goes a long way." My first thought was to picture myself from her point of view. Yes, I did talk a lot. Yes, I did speak in a passionate and opinionated tone. Yes, I sometimes liked being the center of attention and made the best of it. I was crushed and humiliated once I realized that I had many all too human qualities.

I decided to put this knowledge to my advantage. I was going to work harder at listening, rather than expounding. I was going to tone my personality down when around her (since she obviously didn't value it) and most of all I was going to remember that I wasn't the only person in the world. But I also decided that in my defense, I had to realize she was making a statement about herself. I knew the woman to live "on the dark side of the moon". Most of her comments were negative ones about people who were not around to defend themselves. She was always kind and loving to their face but not so when she had an audience and they were absent.

Needing to modify my own behavior was still a reality however. I forced myself to "look behind the scenes" a tool that is often quite useful. What kind of life did this woman have? Was she carrying baggage that contributed to her negativity? She had suffered for many years in a bad marriage followed by a painful and humiliating divorce. She also had a teenage daughter who had been involved in drugs and alcohol and died in a car accident. Another daughter was heavily involved in drugs as well and had given birth to twin boys out of wedlock, then promptly abandoned them to her brother and his wife to raise. The crosses my sister-in-law had to bear may have been of her own choosing or she may have been victimized. In any event, it was easier for me to understand her once I took a hard look at her life. Never hesitate to find out what is going on "behind the scenes."

Some of the platitudes help: Judge not lest ye be judged", "Everyone's right from their point of view", and other similar bits of wisdom. Attempting to put yourself in other's shoes, and understand what might have happened to them to make them the way they are, is a first step. If I do that and still find that what they're doing is unhealthy, not just my opinion, I do my best to keep my mouth shut. Just because I'm right doesn't mean voicing it is a good idea. People make changes in their life only when they're ready and will quite often make none in an attempt to prove they're in control.

I have another interesting story here, about one of my favorite people. I have an adorable and precocious grand-daughter (who has juvenile diabetes and tests her own blood glucose, and gives herself insulin injections—talk about turning a liability into an opportunity to develop character). Emily came home from school one day when she was six years of age and told her mother about a "circle time" they'd had where a friend of hers refused to sit next to a child because he was black. Emily's mother (that'd be my daughter, Cathy) asked her what she did about that. Emily's reply? " I sat down next to him. It's better if I lead by example." Am I proud of that kid or what?

Sometimes, having strong opinions is good. Belief in your own value system (if it's a good one) periodically needs validating. But it still helps to look beyond and behind what someone is doing. Buddy is a friend of my husband's. The first time I met him was when he came to the hospital when I had flown in from California to be with Tom while he was having a pacemaker inserted at the young age of 50. Buddy spent every minute of the next few days sitting in a chair next to Tom, often snoring loudly. But he was always there. He and his lovely wife, Kathleen, gathered me under their wing and took me to their home so I could get some sleep. Buddy is belligerent, a rebel, uses colorful language in the extreme, and makes fun of everyone, including the handicapped. I don't care. It didn't take me long to figure out that behind that façade was the kindest, most devoted man I'd ever known. He grew up in a bad childhood, passed from relative to relative because of parents who didn't care. Sometimes, weighing and balancing a person's value will show you that whatever you may not like about them may be insignificant compared to their contribution to the world.

Being self-absorbed is another toughie. I remember an old joke about a self-centered man who went on and on to a friend about his life, his problems, his opinions, and so on. Finally, he stopped, drew a breath, and said, "Enough about me. What do you think of me?" People who are great listeners are often not self-absorbed, so developing that facet of your character would help you twofold. Focusing on others and learning to hear what they are saying (which just may be more interesting and provide a growing experience) will also contribute to working on this. People who tend to be garrulous usually spend time talking about themselves, something good listeners don't do. Which one do you want to be?

We've talked in an earlier chapter about strong character. It's a lost art. The character of people who lived during the World War II era was forged by the times. But I'm sure that even then the world was populated with weak characters, just as in today's era, there are many who are still strong-charactered that were not born till long after the war. What is happening that honesty, hard work, keeping your word, and showing devotion and fidelity to your mate and family are no longer as valued as they once were? I suspect this issue goes through cycles. In the Roman Empire, the world was full of despots. The French Revolution was brought about by the actions of arrogant and selfish rulers. In our last century, when we all considered ourselves to be more enlightened, more civilized, more progressive than at any other time in history, we also had the most evil of rulers: Hitler,

Mussolini, Pol Pot, and Stalin were only a few. The wars in the 20th century were the most destructive, utilizing the worst of weapons including the atomic bomb. Have we learned nothing? Or is it just a part of life that man will always have its dark side and its side of light. Since Cain and Abel, man has killed man. None of this is new.

How then to deal with it? By taking care of your own little corner of the world, you can make a contribution towards enlightening man and changing the direction of the world. If each person worked on developing, not only their own character but their personal integrity, it would have an impact on others. Choose honesty rather than falsehood; choose hard work instead of laziness; choose devotion and fidelity rather than non-caring and cheating; choose keeping your word rather than betraying yourself. Like my granddaughter Emily, lead by example. It *will* make a difference. Not only will you have a hand in changing the course of mankind for the good, but you will reap the reward of having increased not only your awareness level but your self-esteem.

Wisdom lies in all parts of your day. Life is about growing, about stretching your soul, and becoming not only more than you thought you could, but all that you have a right to be. You *can* move mountains if you want to, one shovel full at a time.

Develop a Sense of Humor

My husband is one of the funniest men I know. He is an exceptionally able cartoonist (still in the closet) and a master at quick wit. With an innate ability to find humor in areas no one else would have thought of, he can keep me in stitches. I often tell him he's my own personal entertainment committee. He came by it naturally and is fortunate in that. Not everyone is so blessed. I have friends who are the "appreciative humor" people (meaning they laugh heartily at anything anyone else says that's funny but are not particularly quick witted themselves) and those who are natural born comedians but not a great audience and those who are talented in both areas.

My father had no sense of humor except when it came to the Dagwood comic strip. On Sunday mornings, his laughter boomed throughout the house as he read about Dagwood's antics. It was almost frightening to us since we weren't used to it at any other time. Our lives were literally sprinkled with commands like "That's not a laughing matter", "No laughing at the dinner table or you'll go to your room", "If you giggle one more time, I'll wash your mouth out with soap", and so on. It was a repressed household at best.

You'd think with that much control going on, my siblings and I would grow up afraid to laugh at anything. Not so. My brother Scott and I have a marvelous sense of humor, laugh freely, make witty comments, and find humor in things other people miss. It wasn't always so. We had to learn over the years to feel safe about laughter. I often wonder if most of the people I know that seem humorless are nothing more than products of a repressed childhood. If you're one of those, sit down and write yourself a letter. Have it come from your parents telling you that you not only have permission to laugh and find humor in your day but it's an order. Read the letter out loud, over and over, every day, until you find yourself believing it.

Start spending more time with people that do have a healthy sense of humor. Learn to laugh at yourself. There is no crime in making mistakes that hurt only you. Laugh at it.

Spend time around small children. Watch them entertain themselves. If that doesn't make you laugh, you're hopeless (and no one's hopeless). I've had more belly laughs from watching my littlest grandchildren, the one to six year olds. They have no pretensions, no artificiality. They will do things to entertain themselves that make you wonder why you didn't think of it yourself.

Our refrigerator is covered with family photos, a large number of them of situations that are hilarious. I have two of Steven and Mark, two grandchildren who were ten and twelve at the time. They are puffing on a cigar and have the most intense "aren't I a grownup" look on their faces (right before they turned green and vowed never to touch the stuff again). Another photo is of Nicholas McKinnon our, at that time, almost three year old. He has nothing on but a pair of bunny slippers. The comment he had just made was "I'm ready to go now." Then there's Nick on all fours playing with his train, buck naked of course. Hunter, my fourteen-year-old grandson, thought it would be funny if I took a photo of both he and Larry, my wonderful son-in-law who's quadriplegic, in wheelchairs so he got the spare to sit in alongside Larry in his automated one. We laughed our heads off at that.

Once we see things in a different light, humor exists every-where.

15 | Financial Dimension

What about our financial dimension? Without wise decisions in this area, we would be living under a bridge. While I have moments when that sounds interesting, the reality is that living on planet earth means we have to provide our bodies with food, clothing, and shelter. That means filling your head with wise choices in this area. If I had to list five rules in the area of our financial dimension that promote good financial health, they would be as follows:

- Curb your spending and learn to live within your income by developing and following a budget.
- Develop a savings and retirement plan.
- Learn to not only respect money and assets but also appreciate and enjoy the fruits they bear; this means setting aside a certain amount for fun.
- Plan ahead.
- We work to earn money. We earn money to enjoy a life style. If you are not happy at your work, find one that you are happy in. If you spend the majority of your waking hours at a job, it should have a certain amount of challenge and enjoyment.

Let's break these rules down and find a way to make them work.

Curb Your Spending by Developing and Following A Budget.

What a drag! A budget? No one does those. Jeeze, it would mean having to think ahead and we certainly don't want to do that. It would mean the *D* word (discipline). Yuk! Sounds like my husband talking. I do budgets. He doesn't. I find it fun. I run a calculator tape every month of what our income will be, then plug in the expenses and get it to balance. I make sure it's realistic, making savings notations for family birthdays and Christmas (so there's no surprise with huge credit card debts after the holidays), travel allocations, regular savings, groceries, insurance, Wal-Mart, etc. etc. I keep an eye on my checkbook balance frequently to see if I've overspent (we're only human), then cut back in another. Any extra money that comes my way, I deposit in my checking account, then immediately make a penciled notation to deduct it and keep a record of it in my savings notation book. I am pleasantly surprised when an expense appears I hadn't planned on that I already have funds put away for. This works for me. It might not for you. Find your own way to have a budget. If you have Microsoft Excel on your computer, it is an excellent way to keep track of what you've spent during the month. More people stress out over finances than anything else. Do you want to be one of them? These are your choices, so make them good.

Develop a Savings and Retirement Plan.

Most people would say, "I don't have enough money the way it is, how can I possibly put money away. It is time for another story.

I grew up in a small town in the Midwest. After twenty-two years, away I returned and fell in love with the area all over again. I renewed friendships, visited farms, and spent a lot of time talking to the friend I was staying with. I went back almost every year to recharge my batteries. One time I was listening to a dear friend of mine who was upset about their financial problems. They were constantly struggling and she didn't know what they were going to do. I found out later, from another friend, to whom I was expressing my concern about the family having financial difficulties, that the only reason they did was because they didn't use their heads. They had a new car every year, their children went to the most expensive universities, and they always had the latest gadgets. I found out that another friend who had more children was doing fine. The reason? They made do with their car for several years before replacing it. The children went to junior colleges and saving for emergencies was more important than having the latest "stuff". I love both women and feel bad for the one having financial difficulties, but more for the fact that she's not using her head.

Another couple I knew years ago had a lovely, expensive home, the latest autos, and both worked for the same company, making six figure incomes each. Then they decided to have a bigger and better, more expensive home custom built. They went deeply into debt but weren't worried because they were going to sell their original home and besides, they made so much money, why worry. After moving into their custom built house, the first home sat on the market month after month with no buyer. Now they were paying on two homes. Then, both of them lost their jobs. They had to file for bankruptcy and within months were living in Arizona where he sold used cars and she worked in a pet store, both of them struggling to put food on the table. Within a year, he had eye cancer and died two years later. The husband had been a childhood friend of mine and to me, it's one of the saddest stories. I don't know that their financial difficulties caused him to develop eye cancer. But I do know that your body only has so many soldiers assigned at birth to fight the many wars it is subject to; colds, flu, diseases, stress etc. When you have to send most of them to "stress battles", you deplete the ones needed to protect not only your immune system but others as well. Just a thought.

Take a hard look at what you spend. Is there a way to consolidate your debts? If you wrote a check to yourself first and put it in your savings, you'd never miss it and after a while, it would be a habit. How about every time you get a raise putting the excess into a savings account? You've been living on the lesser amount until now anyway. It shouldn't be a hardship. All of these behavior changes require not only the desire to make your life healthy in the financial dimension, but take discipline. Even if you're not a disciplined kind of person, you can become one. If you'd rather be in debt and die young from stressing over money woes, that's your choice.

Respect Money and Assets But Also Appreciate and Enjoy It

Now for the good news. No one should be a miser and deprive themselves of the fun benefits in earning an income. Another story. I have a sister and brother-in-law who years ago decided they wanted to move out of the LA area and buy land in Washington State. They yearned to live in the country and raise their four boys in a healthy environment. They started saving for their dream. Paul worked a good job and made decent wages. They saved money by changing their eating habits. Their diet consisted mainly of oatmeal for breakfast, one grilled cheese sandwich for lunch, and a meager casserole for dinner. Their four boys became thin to the point of emaciation.

My son spent the weekend with them once and when he returned, said "never again." He thought he was going to starve. This went on year after year. Fifteen years later, they changed their minds and never moved to Washington. When my father died and left each of his children approximately $70,000, Gretchen loaned half of her inheritance to a friend (and I use this term loosely here) who never repaid it and used the other half to buy a flashy used Lincoln-Continental. I'm not a particularly controlling person (although I'm sure I have my moments—we all do) but there were times when I wanted to shake my sister and tell her to THINK.

Don't deprive yourself of good food. Everyone needs to take at least an annual vacation even if it's only a camping trip. We all have the right to occasionally splurge on something we dearly want. There are ways to spend less on something you want. I frequently buy videos and audios from a company called The Teaching Company. They offer great courses taught by professors from leading universities. I've purchased courses on religion, philosophy, history, literature, and famous people. I just sent away for a video of 36 lectures (30 minutes/lecture) on Victorian Britain. Not only do these courses fascinate me, they enrich my life with knowledge. But I never buy one unless it's on sale. And they all, at one time or another, will go on sale. The one I just bought is originally $300. I bought it for $80. It will bring me many hours of enjoyment.

That may not be of interest to you. But something is. Most of us are possession oriented and spend a certain amount of money on "stuff". Perhaps you'd rather use your money for a movie and dinner once a week or a trip to a museum with lunch afterwards. Everyone spends their money on something. Make your choices the best you can. Set aside an amount in your budget for fun, healthy fun. Then enjoy.

Plan Ahead!

Sometimes, being spontaneous is a wonderful thing. We don't ever want to suffocate the child inside of us. Taking off to go to a movie on the spur of the moment, turning down a road that looks interesting and may have a great hiking trail when it's nowhere on the route to your destination, all of a sudden needing to have an ice cream cone, or shimmying up a tree just because it's there is deeply satisfying. But once in a while (maybe more than that), we need to plan ahead.

When my husband proposed to me, he said he wanted to get married in Scotland. Being the planner that I am, I immediately got on the Internet looking for information on how to make this happen. Tom decided on the location (Melrose, Scotland) but I researched everything from getting the license to hiring a bagpiper to play at the wedding, to planning the reception at a five star hotel, and finishing up by planning a two-week honeymoon starting with our wedding night in a hotel on the shores of Loch Lomond. It was magical, but might not have gone so smoothly had I not planned ahead.

We work to earn money. We earn money to enjoy a lifestyle. If you are not happy at your work, find one that you are happy with. If you spend the majority of your waking hours at a job, it should have a certain amount of challenge and enjoyment.

One of the saddest things I know is how many people work at a job they hate. "Take this job and shove it" is part of a lot of people's daily thoughts. They dream about winning the lottery; they hope someone will rescue them and offer the world's most exciting position. One day, they want to be an author (but no they have never written a book—they think the Leprechauns might do that while they're sleeping).Or maybe they've always yearned to be an architect or a deep-sea diver. I have a friend who recently called and told me that her husband (who had been on a medical leave from the job he hates, giving him lots of time to think) decided he's going back to school to be a paleontologist, something he's always wanted to be. Fortunately, he has a devoted wife who earns good money at a job she likes and is willing to be supportive of him.

There's an old Chinese proverb that goes something like this: If you want to be happy for a day, go fishing; if you want to be happy for a week, take a vacation; if you want to be happy for a month, get married; and if you want to be happy for life, enjoy your work.

This is another one of those easy-for-you-to-say comments. Most people fall into their jobs, never intending to spend their life at it, only to wake up thirty years later and find they hated it. I have another dear friend who has worked as a scrub nurse for forty years at the same hospital. After 35 years, her hands were so badly damaged from constant washing that she had to begin doing clerical work or else lose her job. After forty years, she has no pension (they have no retirement plan, almost unbelievable) and no medical benefits if she retires. She will have to work till she can collect social security but says she's a hard worker and doesn't mind. I can't help but think that some part of her must be angry.

So what should you do if you're one who hates their job? Take the time to think about what you'd rather be doing. Research the possibilities of perhaps going back to school to get a degree in what you might need to become what you want to. Student loans, grants, junior colleges, and so on are more available than you think. Check with the company you work for. Many corporations are now funding education for their employees. If you want to do something bad enough, just put the dream in front of you and you'll get there. Be realistic. If you're 52 and want to be the President of the United States but have never even slightly been involved in politics, there's a good chance you might be better off with a second choice. Ditto if you're 60 and want to be a rock star. You have to at least use common sense.

Most of us have more than one thing we'd like to do for a living. Maybe you always wanted to be a landscaper but here you are working at a machine shop. How about checking the local nurseries to see if they need a part time worker? You can check books out of the library about the subject and become as educated as anyone who went to college. Maybe you could start by doing some landscaping in your own yard, take pictures, and put up flyers to see if anyone would like to hire you to do their yard.

All you need is to know what you want to be (when you grow up) and what direction to go in. Everything else will come together.

I want to give one final word about financial success. It is only a small part in achieving contentment in life. I have a coffee cup that reads, "Money can't buy happiness but it can sure make being miserable a lot more fun." Obviously having enough income to be comfortable brings more stability and happiness in life than being poverty stricken. One of the unfortunate truths is that it takes an income to maneuver through it with some success. But this realization must be balanced with truth. Too many people make the mistake of thinking if they only won the lottery, if only Uncle Jack would die and leave them that money, if only their boss would give them a huge raise, then they would be happy.

Think of the wealthy heiress Barbara Hutton and you will more fully realize that the old adage of "money can't buy happiness" is true. Her life was one of mostly neurotic unhappiness and joyless rushing from one moneyed event to another. At the end of her life, she lived in so much apathy that she had to be carried to any place she needed to go. If that poor woman had spent her millions helping others, building educational foundations, and setting up trusts for research, her life would have had a purpose. She would have discovered that outside her own insatiable needs waited a world of fulfillment and joy. Picture Howard Hughes. With all his money, he lay in an eccentric stupor at the end of his life, buried in a paranoid existence where he was terrified of death. How sad to see that those who have so much in material resources lack the very spiritual foundation needed to give them a meaningful life!

16 | The Vowel Syndrome

Now that you've learned something about growth through a path of positive energy in the areas of the six dimensions, I'm going to give you a tool, one that can be used in all six areas to enrich your life even further. I call it the *Vowel Syndrome* .

Most people think that living a successful life means achieving goals. It is much more than that. Using the vowels, you can discover that it encompasses all of the following:

A - *a*ppreciate

E - *e*xperience

I - *i*nvestigate

O - *o*bserve

U - *u*nderstand

I offer up these five relatively unimportant letters as a guide because once we commit them to memory, it will be easy to continually access them in all avenues of life, especially in the areas of the six dimensions. Let's start by seeing what our friend Webster says about them and then explore each further.

Appreciate

- To grasp the nature, worth, quality, or significance of; to value or admire highly.
- To judge with heightened perception or understanding.
- To be fully aware of, to recognize with gratitude.

How many times do we have an experience that we only feel on the surface? A friend may be telling us about something that happened in their life and we only give lip service: "Is that right? How nice," etc. It's often only later that we realize we didn't fully appreciate what they were trying to share. The trite saying about "smell the roses" has much significance. People who are detail-oriented often experience so much more than those of us who rush through something so we can be at the next experience waiting for us.

Experience

- Direct observation of, or participation in, events as a basis of knowledge.

It's not sufficient to be in the space of an experience. What can we learn from it that will contribute greatly to our lives? Much wisdom lies in looking back at our experiences, especially the ones where we stub our toe, so to speak. How can we keep from repeating this? Wear shoes, watch your feet, and so on. Everything that happens in our lives contains gems of knowledge that can be turned to wisdom, wisdom that can mean the difference between being happy and being bitter.

Investigate

- To study by close examination and systematic inquiry.

How many of us have watched a squirrel scamper up a bird feeder, perch precariously on its edge, and fill their little cheeks to the brim? How often have you seen a caterpillar creep across a twig or how about a Monarch butterfly flitting from flower to flower? Doesn't it raise questions about where the squirrels take their food once they've filled their pouch? Don't you wonder how long it will be before the caterpillar becomes a Monarch butterfly or how long the butterfly will live? Children have a natural curiosity about these things but as adults, we lose our capacity to investigate further, to ask questions. Our "need to know" becomes blunted by day-to-day worries. We lose our ability to find enchantment in our entire universe.

Once I completed recovery, I found myself wondering why the sea changed colors as I drove up the Pacific Coast Highway (Since I mentioned this previously, it's obvious this drive contained memorable experiences). In Los Angeles, it was the color of steel, in Santa Barbara it was a pearly gray, in Carmel and Monterey it had become a deep green, and by the time I arrived in the Redwood and the wine country, it had changed to an azure blue. Why, I wondered? These questions prompted me to research and I found that the depth of the water had a great bearing on its color. A questioning mind seeks relief in books, discussion, the Internet, or any other source it can find to enrich itself with the discovery of more knowledge. How much more satisfying a drive up the coast is to me, now that I've learned more about the colors of the ocean?

Observe

- To watch carefully with attention to details or behavior, for the purpose of arriving at a judgment.

The word *judgment* has received a bad rap. According to our friend, Webster, (ask me how many dictionaries I have in my home) it is the act or process of the mind in comparing its ideas to find their agreement or disagreement, and to ascertain truth; the process of examining facts and arguments to ascertain propriety and justice. It is also the ability to come to opinions of things; the power to compare ideas and ascertain the relations of terms and propositions.

It is only harsh, cruel, or negative judgments that are not good. Once you couple observations with the below vowel of understanding, you arrive at the truth.

Understand

- To achieve a grasp of the nature, significance, or explanation of something.

In my belief system, understanding is one of the greater gifts humans have been given. When combined with wisdom, it brings peace and personal power.

Before Tom and I moved to Arizona, my eldest daughter Cathy arrived in Colorado with her sibling Tammie and six grandchildren in tow for a week's vacation with Tom and me. As a result of something called "restless leg syndrome", the product of too much stress buildup, I had been having a great deal of difficulty with burning feet and thereby, insomnia. It created more negative energy in me than I was comfortable with. I mentioned this to my daughter several times while she was visiting so that she wouldn't take it personally. I had also discussed with her the difficulties I'd had in the last two years in adjusting to all the changes that moving to Colorado had entailed.

Cathy, detail-oriented, is by nature a critical person, just part of her makeup, her resident human frailty. She has other marvelous qualities that make up for it. She is a natural giver, has a brilliant mind, a marvelous sense of humor, is a wonderful wife and mother, and extremely devoted to her siblings and her mother. She is also a two-time Emmy Award winner as a sound editor for Warner Brothers. All this from a young lady who, several years ago, admitted herself to Sierra Tucson, a recovery center in Arizona, for thirty days to overcome alcoholism and bulimia. She recently celebrated her fourteenth year of sobriety and not only works with recovering alcoholics on a daily basis, but also has begun an innovative meeting for Twelve Steppers that provides childcare.

On the last day of her visit, Cathy and I were sitting on the outdoor swing. I made a comment about the bird feeder on the pole not being straight and how it bugged me. I followed that up with the innocent question, "When had I gotten so fussy?" Cathy's response startled me. "I've been meaning to talk to you about that mom. I've noticed that you've become judgmental and negative and I'm concerned about how unhappy it's making you. You seem to think that everyone has to have the same opinions you do or else they're not okay. "

Quite startled, since I hadn't seen her comments coming, I responded, "I can certainly be opinionated and I'm also verbal so when you combine that with sleep deprivation, I'm probably going to come across as more negative and judgmental than usual." I asked her to give me some "for instances" so I could see what she was talking about but she didn't want to discuss it any further.

The old pre-recovery me would have burst into tears, become defensive and angry at my beloved daughter. I was elated that the new me had tools to draw on to bring about a less painful response. First of all, I told myself I'd look at my own behavior and see if there was any truth in her words. Once done, I'd take steps to correct it. If there was nothing there, I would move away from any possible hurt by reminding myself that while I'm opinionated (which can be offensive to people), Cathy looks at people's behavior through a magnifying glass and is more comfortable when she's in control of everything in her universe. We tease her about alphabetizing her groceries. I still loved her unconditionally and decided not to take offense at her remark and also, not to bring it up again.

The day may come when she will realize she judged me harshly or the day may come when I realize there was more truth in her words than I originally thought. Or I may even choose to decide that the entire exchange was not important enough to give much attention to. I also used my husband as a sounding board (if you have a healthy and honest relationship with your mate, this can be a great tool) to see whether he thought I'd better do some "fixing". I have to admit to feeling elated when he saw no signs of that sort of behavior in me and was confused at Cathy's comments.

Understanding the situation, thereby bringing a more global perspective to the exchange (which always helps), gave me a sense of peace and personal power where anger and defensiveness would have left me shaking and depressed.

A couple of days later I was watching *The Philadelphia Story* (1940), and paid close attention to Cary Grant's speech to Katherine Hepburn about her character's inability to accept human frailties in others. I found myself thinking about this a lot the rest of the day. Part of being human is knowing the frailties we have (and we all *do* have them) and part of being divine is our ability to understand and accept these frailties, not only in ourselves but also in others.

Living fully is not just about being in a certain space. It's about appreciating all that space encompasses. The deeper you experience something, the more value it will have, not just as a learning experience, but also as a pleasure experience. I mentioned in an earlier chapter about a part of my philosophy encompassing both pleasure and purpose. I believe that is the reason we are alive. A life with dutiful purpose but no pleasure is not a balanced life and a life with only pleasure has no direction and no reason for existence. Using the vowel syndrome you can, not only enhance the value of your own life, but also discover new voyages, new adventures and new pleasures and purposes.

Sudden Death and Other Changes

If we're going to become healthy in the area of the six dimensions, we are going to have to understand change. It is a part of life. Like death and taxes, it is inevitable. Any resistance to change is perfectly normal. It is only how we accept it that makes the difference in change being traumatic or exciting.

Most of the changes we go through are minor, a new mail man on our route comes at an inconvenient time for us; a change of receptionist at the doctor's office puts us in a surly mood since she's not as familiar with our life as the other one; a new boss comes on to the scene when we loved the old one; a local highway construction project forces us through a detour in an unpleasant part of town. Even supermarkets seem to be in on it. They regularly change the location of their stock right after we become so familiar with it that we could wander through the store blindfolded and still pick out our purchase.

As infants, we begin to adjust to minor changes with regularity. They soon become a part of our life. Some feel good, such as a raise in our allowance. Others, a new teacher who is the dreaded Mrs. Murray, brings not so pleasant ones. But we adjust. We adjust because we understand unconsciously that change is a part of life. When it becomes more painful than we are willing to accept, it is now not something we like.

Most of us are forced at one time or another to go through large changes through no fault of our own. The company where we've been employed for over twenty years changes hands and begins layoffs. We are a part of that change and it comes as a loss equal to a death. An elderly parent dies and even though we've had our moments of anger with them, they are now no longer a part of our predictable and orderly life. We feel the loss more painfully than we had expected to. Our perspective on the part they played in our life changes. We no longer see the reality of how difficult they may have been. Death softens any bad behavior patterns. Our sense of guilt that we are alive and they are not compounds the problem of trying to adjust to the change. If that parent was one that we enjoyed and had no problems with, now the difficulty in adjusting multiplies. There is always a sense of loss with change. It is frightening and we lose our balance, our confidence, and our feeling of well-being.

I had a co-worker many years ago that came home with her family from a month's vacation to find that her house had burned to the ground, no belongings salvageable at all. She and her husband had been married twenty-five years and the accumulation of family mementos, gifts, and necessary items was enormous. As they had been camping, no one had been able to contact them and let them know in advance what had happened to cushion their blow. Despite receiving a large amount of insurance money, more than enough to cover their losses, my co-worker was so devastated that she was off work for a month, unable to cope with the slightest daily routine. Even now, years later, she still feels the shock and grief. One can hardly blame her. My heart goes out to those whose mate came home one day and announced they were leaving. How does one cope with the enormity of such a change, especially if it is unexpected?

One of the most interesting experiences with change happened to me. At the age of fifty-eight, I transferred from the Los Angeles area to Colorado to work in the Sales Department of an HMO, after almost a decade of working in Preventive Medicine. After several years of being single, I married a small town guy who lived in the Colorado Rockies in a town with less than a hundred people and sold a lovely home I'd owned for fourteen years to move into his mountain cabin half the size of my home in LA. This necessitated putting my belongings in storage for a year and a half while we waited for the completion of a remodel. I had left my four children whom I had an extremely close relationship with, my eleven grandchildren, ditto, numerous friends, and a women's writer's group that I cherished deeply. I had exchanged a lifestyle that included attending cultural events, traveling around the world, indulging my passion for movies, regular get togethers with friends for meals, dancing, and whatever pleasure struck my fancy for a lonely life in the woods, no friends other than my husband and any hope of attending movies and cultural events more of a hardship than I cared to assume.

I learned a lot in the first ten months.

I learned that it takes time more than anything to adjust to the changes. I had never realized what anchor points the familiarity of possessions, of routines and of people could become in one's life. My husband's mountain home had lovely belongings, filled with mostly antiques and "male energy stuff" such as guns, motorcycles, paintings of wolves, and lots and lots of model cars, trains and, of course, more motorcycles. I liked all of them but they weren't my "stuff". I suffered through crying jags on a weekly basis, ones where all I seemed to say over and over was, "what have I done?"

Intellectually, I knew I'd made the right choice. I loved Tom McKinnon and with every fiber in me, I knew he was the man I was meant to grow old with. But emotionally

I missed my family, my friends, my belongings that now languished in two ten by ten storage units, and I especially missed my lovely home. Now, despite knowing that I'd done the right thing, I was like a child who had lost her parent. I grieved on a continual basis.

The fact that as a child my parents had moved from one town to another, while my father followed the work in a construction gang, only contributed to my sense of loss. My whole life, I'd yearned for a place to grow roots. I'd done that in LA and now yanked them out again. When we grieve the loss of someone or something, whether through death or change, it reverberates to all the losses we've felt throughout our life, in particular the ones from our childhood.

The enormity of my difficulty in adjusting to all the changes was fully realized one day when, while in Denver, I approached a signal that was red. Just before the point at which I should have stepped on the brakes, I found my mind going totally blank with any familiarity. I didn't know who I was; where I was; or even that stopping was essential when a signal changed to red. I literally developed, for a few seconds, total amnesia. The result was a head on collision in the midst of the intersection. Thankfully, neither the woman in the other car nor I was injured, but my car was totaled. Too many changes all at one time can be extremely damaging, not only physically, like mine were, but emotionally, mentally, spiritually, socially, and financially. This is all the more reason to stay as healthy as possible in all areas of those six dimensions. You never know what changes are going to be hurled your way and you'll need the stabilizing force of healthy dimensions in order to cope.

A few basic rules about going through so many major changes would have helped me. I can see, looking back, that giving myself time to adjust was an absolute requirement. It doesn't happen overnight and everyone is different in how long it does take. I expected to feel wonderful about my new life as soon as I got there. I gave myself no room to slowly slip into everything. Had I known that help was on the way by being patient, I could have accepted the grieving I was going through more easily. And grieving it was.

I also didn't realize, in my new found love, that I needed to cut both Tom and I some slack in discovering the reality of who and what we were. My shortcomings were quickly evident to him and vice versa. We're all only human and near as I can tell the only perfect person was crucified. I went slowly in making changes in my new home. Tom didn't take change easily and even moving some of my kitchen utensils in to the house had to be done in a one step at a time manner.

In time, we adjusted to each other and almost had to fall in love all over again. We acquired new wisdom, tolerance, and a depth of feeling we hadn't realized would happen. It was as if in going through the tough times, we forged an even stronger bond. In time, I learned to adopt new routines that became familiar and helped with the pinch of missing old ones. I learned to compensate for not having close friends nearby by making more phone calls, sending cards and emails, and by looking forward to frequent visits to California.

Even death, which stalks us on a continual basis, once we go through the grieving, can bring a change in our life that's been long overdue. This is not to say that we don't grieve the parting of the loved one. When one loses a grandparent who has lived a long life, it is, nevertheless, painful. If we lose a child, it can be a lifelong agony of remembering one that is almost impossible to go beyond. But we all have our time to leave, and death, like minor changes in our life, brings a time of leave taking. Since I believe that we are a soul with a body, not a body with a soul, in my moments of maturity, I recognize that even the loss of my little sister, Jeanne, was a part of life that I had no control over. I will miss her until I die. But I feel her in my heart on a daily basis. So she is not gone; she has only changed, and is in her soul form.

Change is much like that. We never lose anything. Sometimes we just give it back. Ultimately, when change comes to our life, we are responsible for our own attitude. We can take ownership of it; we can be patient; we can develop a sense of humor; we can practice stress management techniques and we can create our own future instead of grieving over the past. There are things you can control and things you can't. Remember the Serenity Prayer: **God grant me the serenity to accept the things I cannot change, the courage to change the things I can and the wisdom to know the difference.** Keep in mind that the majority of changes bring growth and that without growth, we die, if not physically but mentally, spiritually, emotionally, socially, and financially.

It has been said that there are four stages of change:

- Oblivion – act as if it's not there and maybe it'll go away.
- Rebellion – if I fight this, maybe I won't have to go through it.
- Motivation – you begin to gather information on why you are going through the change.
- Acceptance

Keep in mind that no matter how drastic the change, you will eventually achieve that fourth step.

A few rules to help you adjust to change, once you know it is coming, will go a long way to easing your discomfort. Read these rules, over and over, until you have adjusted.

- Be patient. In time, all that is now unfamiliar will become familiar.
- If the change was brought about by your own choice and you thought it out thoroughly beforehand and made the decision that it was the right choice for you, then, just know that in time, you will bear the fruit of your own wisdom.
- Remember that you can control your own emotional reaction to the changes. You don't have to be fearful unless you choose to.

- If you had no choice in the change but it was in fact thrust upon you, keep the Serenity Prayer in mind. In my opinion, it is one of the most powerful prayers ever written and repeated over and over, and will give you strength.

- Expect a sense of loss with any change, even if your change is for the better.

- Make the changes work for you in a positive manner.

- Do not make any more major changes than you have to. You are already going through enough.

- Make a list of the things in your life that have not changed. Focus on them frequently and utilize them as stability points in your life.

I close this chapter with the following words, a poem I wrote while going through recovery.

CHANGE

Change has always loomed,
Like a demon in my mind,
It pounces sharp on all my plans,
The treasures that I find,
I hate it when it comes to me,
A smile upon its face,
Disguised in goodness and character,
Dressed up in pearls and lace.
My life is set in front of me,
Predictable and fast,
How dare this wayward, orphan child,
Stray me from my task.
It flounders, wanders, oscillates,
With its persistent, nagging voice,
Bent upon surprising me,
With growth and will and choice,

But I can see through all of this,
This aim to tempt my fate,
And call adventure to my door,
When I'd really rather wait,
For deep inside my cautious heart,
Lurks a frightened child,
Who doesn't know if she can cope,
When change makes her riled,
What if I stumble, lose my way,
Fall and skin my knee?
What if life, that brings this change,
Becomes an obstacle to me?
But I must play the advocate,
With deep humility,
I must admit that without change,
I'm never really free.

How about giving change a chance? You'll never know what magic is waiting for you until you do.

18	**Fear**

Some of the truest words ever spoken were Franklin Delano Roosevelt's "We have nothing to fear, but fear itself." They carried a nation through the worst time in its history, gave them courage when they didn't think they had it. When you think about these words, there is a lot of truth there. Fear, mostly a learned experience, not an experience by nature, follows almost everyone throughout his or her life. It starts in infancy when a child realizes its mother has left the room and they are in their crib alone. It carries through as toddlers when we take our first steps and fall. It grows when we hear words like, "Watch out, you'll get hurt!" Or, "Be careful, that's dangerous". Sometimes, those warnings were true, like when we reached towards the fire; and sometimes, they were just an extension of the fear of the person who said the words. Fear follows us to school, through trepidation at losing our first friend, the first time we fell out of a tree when we thought we were invincible, and to the doctor's office when we received our first shots.

Speaking of getting shots, I want to share an interesting story about fear. When I was in the first grade in North Dakota, we were all told to go down to the gymnasium where we were going to get shots. None of us were sure what a shot was; only that it hurt and had something to do with a needle. That was scary enough, but standing in a long line with other fearful faces made it worse. There was one brave soul in front of me, a boy who looked at us with disdain as he proclaimed, "I can't believe you're afraid of a silly little needle."

"Aren't you?" we asked.

"Not at all," he stated with another look down his nose at his cowardly classmates.

When his turn came, he passed out cold and had to be carried to the nurse's office. So much for courage vs. fear.

I remember as a pre-adolescent in the mid-west spending many happy hours at the local community swimming pool; with one exception. Despite being terrified of heights, I was always compelled to climb the ladder to the high dive, wait with quivering legs for my turn, look behind me at the long line of confident divers waiting behind me, realize I had no choice but to go forth, and did so with my heart beating battle drums in my head as I closed my eyes and jumped. I'd hit the water like a shock wave, my body plunging to the bottom of the pool, then float quickly to the top, climb out of the pool, and go right back to stand in line. I did this fearful act over and over every time I was at the pool, never quite sure why.

Looking back, I can only assume I was testing myself, each time hoping that I would be less fearful. I still do that. When I was in post recovery, I read a popular book. Once again, all I really needed was the title: *Feel the Fear and Do It Anyway*. In time, I came to realize that fear contained many components. Fear is a motivator, fear is a protector, and fear is an incentive. Mainly, fear propels us into the mainstream of life. To an athlete, fear is adrenalin; to a race car driver or a mountain climber, fear is the incentive to display courage. The other side of fear is just that. When I was in recovery, I penned the following words (the ones that prompted such disdain in fellow would-be authors):

> Courage has a purpose, in our lives I'm told,
> It bonds us with adversity, puts anxiety on hold.

All the choices made, all the rules we bend,
Sure must have a meaning. Is it fear whose fires we tend?
Every day that passes, brings another test.
That we must confront to see which choice is best,
For surely none of us, wants the other one to know,
That somewhere lurks a coward deep inside our soul,
So all of us pretend that such brave hearts are we,
Never realizing, what we fake, will someday be.

Many times in my life, I've found that by simply pretending something, I was able to make it a reality. This is often true when overcoming fear. Courage is the only antidote for fear and whether we realize or not, we all have it. Most of us have never had it tested. How many times have we heard stories about superhuman strength in little old ladies when they needed to save the life of a loved one? Only mental negativity keeps us from utilizing our courage to its fullest extent. If you tell yourself often enough, "I can't do that," guess what? Your mind thinks you've just given it an instruction. Like the little engine that could, we all can. Again, it's the size of the carrot that decides the success or failure of a dream.

When I was eight years old, my family visited Finnish relatives in northern Minnesota. One of them included my Uncle Wally. Uncle Wally was five feet, four inches, and had given bullying a new name. He was impatient and hard-nosed, bellowing, threatening, and insulting his way through family gatherings. In short (pardon the pun), he did anything that intimidated people. I was terrified of him. One day he herded the smaller ones of our group into his car to drive to a nearby town to get ice cream for the family gathering. I wound up sitting in the front seat and after Uncle Wally had circled the block many times, trying to find a parking spot and now in a bad temper, he double parked in front of the ice cream parlor, handed me some money, and told me to go in and get a gallon of vanilla ice cream. Timid to the point of catatonic, at least around my Uncle Wally, I slunk my way out of the front seat and clutching the dollar bills made my way into the store, my heart pounding so loud that I felt everyone in the store could hear it. I stood at the back of the milling crowd of customers, hoping they would soon disperse and I'd be able to buy the ice cream.

Within minutes, my arm was being yanked and I heard Uncle Wally's voice bellowing in my ear. "Why haven't you bought the ice cream yet?"

I stuttered apologies and excuses as he dragged me through the crowd pushing his way and knocking people rudely aside.

"A gallon of vanilla ice cream," he stated loudly as he grabbed the money out of my hand and plopped it on the counter.

The clerk took the money and immediately handed him the ice cream.

As we pushed our way back out of the store, Uncle Wally, still holding my arm firmly, said, "You'll never get anywhere in life with a faint heart." His philosophy was correct if not his behavior. This event stood out in my mind over the years. Uncle Wally, like a lot of short people, had learned to compensate for his lack of height by adopting an intimidating manner. While I've never felt an intimidating manner was appropriate behavior, I do see the wisdom of not having a faint heart.

19 | Maintaining Optimism in the Face of Adversity

Now that we've talked about fear, let's talk about ways to maintain optimism in the face of adversity.

Trying to keep a "stiff upper lip" is not easy for some of us. Others seem to be born with it. The British are a classic example. Despite going through the horrors of the London Blitz during World War II, they maintained a normalcy to their life that was unflappable. Many families sent their children to the country to keep them out of harm's way, sometimes not seeing them for months at a time while they tried to carry on as usual. It's pretty difficult to swallow terror when air raid sirens go off and you must race to a shelter soon or wind up dead. They often spent hours in these shelters listening to bombs falling overhead, shrill whistling noises followed by deafening explosions, never knowing what they'd find once they crept out of the shelter. The Brits are not only famous for their optimism in adversity but along with that, the dry humor they draw on to buffer themselves has forged impeccable character.

Kathleen Ainsley, my dear friend (and a Brit) and Maid of Honor when Tom and I were married in Scotland, has the traditional British upper lip. Her first child, Matthew, was born with Down's Syndrome. It was heartbreaking for Kathleen and her husband Paul, who was Tom's Best Man. But with typical British intestinal fortitude and a no-nonsense attitude, she said, "Well, you just carry on, after all, don't you." She and Paul have never once felt sorry for themselves and have indeed "carried on". Tom and I find Matthew an enchanting child and I have no doubt that part of his remarkable personality is due to having exemplary parents.

The wonderful benefit in maintaining optimism in the face of adversity is how it makes you feel so good about yourself and how well it prepares you for anything down the road that may be unpleasant. There is no escaping what I call the "Cain and Abel" syndrome. Since the beginning of man's known history, there has been good and evil. Dark is followed by light and then again by dark. Life has always been this way and will continue in the same vein forever. For those who moan about the magnitude of evil and wars in the twentieth century, I offer only that Genghis Khan, despotic Roman emperors, and a number of British and French monarchs contributed greatly to the cruelty of the world in earlier centuries. Even religion, which is responsible for more deaths than anything, cannot escape being one of the guilty culprits (How about the Spanish Inquisition?) Man will always make war on man and the world will always be filled with both good and evil people. We can do little to change the primary course of mankind. But we can change our little corner of the world by maintaining optimism no matter what trials are sent our way. By becoming stronger on a daily basis, we prepare ourselves for unpleasant events that are beyond our control.

On the morning of September 11th, 2001, while at work, I discovered my wallet was missing. Before calling to have all my credit cards cancelled and my checking account closed, I decided to call my home where our contractors were in the middle of a major remodel. I figured I'd probably dropped it in the bedroom and they would locate it for me and all would be well. Jim, one of the carpenters, answered the phone.

"Jim, I think I dropped my wallet in the bedroom this morning. Would you check for me to see if you can locate it?"

"I'd be glad to." His voice was tense and that statement was followed by another. "Did you hear a plane crashed into the World Trade Center?"

Vaguely, I wondered where the World Trade Center was and thought briefly about all the private pilots that didn't know what they're doing. "Really." The plane crashing into the World Trade Center left my mind and I added, "I think it's probably next to the bed on the right side. That's my side. Take a look."

I could hear Jim walking through the house with the cordless phone. "It blew up the tower and now there's another plane heading for it. Oh, my God, hold on a minute."

I could hear the noise of their boom box in the distance blasting out the news. "Jim, check the computer room too. If it's not in the bedroom, I might have left it in there....or maybe on the counter in the kitchen. It's bound to be somewhere."

"No, I can't find it. Oh, this is awful. My God!"

"What? Did you find it?"

I think about the above scenario a lot. Everyone in America will, like at the moment we heard of Kennedy's assassination, know exactly what they were doing at the moment when the terrorists set off the horror that happened on September 11. In my case, I was being a selfish idiot. Later, I spoke with my eldest daughter Cathy. She had just dropped her five-year-old off for her first day at kindergarten and was talking to some other parents when a janitor walked up and said, "Did you hear a plane just hit the World Trade Center?"

Cathy's response was an irritated "That's a pretty sick joke to be telling people around little kids."

"It's not a joke."

How many of us wandered through that day in stunned disbelief, thinking this can't be happening. Not in America. During those tragic hours and the many days that followed, all we wanted was for someone to tell us it was a bad joke. Barring that, we wanted to be children again, and believe that nothing bad ever happens to people, at least not while we had a mom and a dad to protect us.

How many times in life have we had to face adversity, if not something that we only hear about that jolts us into fear and uncertainty, such as the terrorist's attacks of September 11, perhaps something that touches us in a much closer manner. Many, not only the ones that died that day, were directly affected in ways in which their world would never be well again. The wives of the gallant firefighters, the parents of the people killed and maimed, the children who lost their fathers and the wives and husbands who lost their mates—would for the rest of their lives walk in dark shadows. Even once the shock wore out and the grief ran its course and the healing entered their hearts, there would still be pain.

My little sister was killed in 1977 but I can still hardly bear to think of her without a wrenching pain that knocks me to my knees. I handle it by not thinking about it, by putting a film of white cotton between the memory and myself, viewing it, if I need to, from a distance of time. It remains painful, nonetheless.

So how does one deal with adversity? There are a hundred sayings to prop you up. **When the going gets tough, the tough get going,** is but one along the theme that reminds us that those of us with character will survive. It's the others that have a tough

time. A friend of mine once said that he could always tell whether a person was of strong character or not by the kind of decisions they made. When faced with two choices, a strong-charactered person will always choose the tough decision. A weak-charactered person will find the easy way out. The sad part about this is that one only becomes weaker as time goes on when that is your choice. For those who make the tough choices, life becomes easier. I'm not saying that in making tough decisions, you will someday have an end to adversity. There is no end to adversity. That is life. But once you have developed what is referred to, in an old fashioned manner, as "intestinal fortitude," you will feel the surge of power that always accompanies having courage.

To begin with, when faced with adversity, whether indirectly affected by the kind we were all a part of on September 11, or directly impacted by, say the death of a loved one, it's important to keep your balance. It's okay to feel the emotional pain. Feeling is a release and a necessary part of coping skills. I had a mother-in-law once who, when her husband was hospitalized after a stroke, answered the phone one night while her grown children were gathered around. After speaking on the phone for a couple minutes, she hung it up, went to the closet, and took out a pail and sponge. The children watched in amazement as she filled the pail with soapy water, placed the sponge in it and began washing the kitchen walls. When asked who was on the phone, she replied that it was the hospital and that their father had just died. They thought she had lost her mind. When I heard the story, I knew that wasn't true. She was attempting to maintain her balance.

One of the gems of wisdom that has helped me a lot in my journey through life is something my mother told me when I was very young; a phrase we've all heard over and

Over, but tend to take for granted: **This too shall pass.** Look back on your life and you'll see that everything bad that has ever happened to you was softened by the passage of time. You either learned to live with whatever repercussions came from your particular challenge, or you learned to make choices to improve your life as a result of it. Maybe you were fortunate enough to realize that the event you perceived as a tragedy turned out to be one of the best things that could have happened to you.

I've used my son-in-law, Larry, as an example many times in this book. Here was a young man who had what almost everyone would have perceived as the greatest tragedy a human could experience, an auto accident that left him a quadriplegic. And yet, a scant dozen years or so after his accident, he works a full-time job as a purchasing agent. He drives a specially equipped van, owns a beautiful home, travels extensively, and has fathered the greatest joy of his life, my grandson Nicholas McKinnon. When I have a problem, I call Larry. He may be partially paralyzed but it has prompted him to develop further his ability to resolve a problem. Do you think he achieved this without maintaining optimism in the face of adversity?

Now, a word about his wife, my youngest daughter, Teri. When Teri was seventeen years old, she was raped at gunpoint by a masked bandit while she was working at a fast food restaurant. After raping her, he put the gun to her head and said, "I'm going to blow your fucking brains out." Instead, he ran out the door. She survived the tragedy but it left deep scars. She could have turned to alcohol or drugs to wipe out the memory. Instead, she became a Registered Nurse so that she could help others. She has saved lives in ER, Surgery, Pediatrics, and PCU. She has delivered babies in the Nursery and handled violent criminals in Detention Care.

When she and Larry's son, Nicholas (created through *in vitro* fertilization), was about to enter this world, Larry was driving his van to the hospital while Teri was in the back seat in labor. Two of my other grandchildren were in the front with Larry. Hunter, ten years old at the time, was on the phone with the Emergency Department at the hospital, where they were headed. All of a sudden, Nicholas decided to make an appearance on his own. Teri put her hands out in front of her as he came sliding out and caught him. Her words to me later were, "What else was I supposed to do, Mom?" Teri could have chosen a life of feeling sorry for herself. It isn't that she doesn't have triggers that recreate the trauma she went through. She has many. But she chose instead to channel her fear into an occupation where she can make a positive impact on other lives. She has evolved into a bright, funny, and extremely wise young lady who genuinely enjoys being one of the best nurses I've ever known.

To add to this happy story is another. Michael, Hunter, and Katie Montana, Teri's children by a previous marriage, are in the process of becoming not only productive, wise, and under-standing humans, but as a result of being around Larry, they have already achieved a nobility that few people arrive at. By instinct, they reach out to help others; they understand human frailties and they are incredibly tolerant and non-judgmental. All of this is a result of being in Larry's life. He needs them to do things for him that he is unable to do for himself. In return, he drives Katie to her dance class; he takes Hunter to soccer games; and helps Michael with computer issues.

A few years ago, I took Hunter and Katie camping with a friend of mine who also had two of her grandchildren. As soon as we pulled up in camp, without me saying a word to them, Katie began unpacking the car and Hunter assembled the tent. Afterwards, they gathered firewood. My friend's grandchildren sat down on a nearby picnic bench and waited for their grandmother to do all the work and wait on them. The entire weekend went like that. I was extremely proud and also aware that in knowing Larry, my grandchildren have received a priceless gift.

I have previously mentioned two of my children, Cathy and Teri, who are contributing to the world in a positive manner. A quick word about the other two. My ex-husband sexually abused Tammie, my second eldest daughter (Cathy was also sexually abused). She spent ten years living on a reservation in a severely abusive marriage to an American Indian. Today, she is married to a wonderful and healthy man and after working many years as a psych tech at a hospital for the criminally insane (boy do we have interesting conversations at family gatherings), she quit going back to school to become a teacher. On a daily basis, she made contributions to the well-being of the unfortunate. Even now, while going to school, she is in charge of a student exchange program every summer. So you can see that, despite four out of four family members being victims of childhood sexual abuse, they have all turned their lives around. For those who feel hopeless from similar situations, this sounds like awesome (and obtainable) statistics to me.

My son, Michael, was on the LAPD for over fifteen years. Upon graduating from the academy, he made the statement to me, "Maybe I can make a difference, Mom." He worked in several divisions: Patrol, Gang, Detective, Narcotics, and Robbery. After the LA riots of a few years ago, his comment was: "I'm probably the only police officer on the LAPD who still enjoys being a cop". In 1998, he was awarded the title of "Officer of the Year." Today, he is in Afghanistan, working for the State Department to train police officials in the use of weapons.

I make these statements about my children, not to have an opportunity to brag (although that's certainly true) but to illustrate that four human beings who came from an alcoholic father, an abusive and alcoholic step-father, and a mother who spent many years screwed up from childhood abuse, including suicide attempts and nervous breakdowns, were able to create meaningful and productive lives. I'd like to take the credit but personally, I think it's their own doing. There is no excuse for anyone, no matter what their childhood, to create their own perfect world once they become adults. Hopefully, if you haven't done that yet, this book will help you.

20 Letting Go

One thing I learned while living alone is that your bad behavior patterns go unnoticed by anyone but you. I was sharply reminded of this after I'd been married to Tom for several months. I was also reminded, one more time, that recovery is a lifelong process. Letting go is also a large part of good mental health.

It all came about regarding obsessive behavior, that persistent disturbing pre-occupation with an often-unreasonable idea or feeling. While trying to heal from childhood trauma, you discover that obsessing on something or someone is a daily part of your life. How do you let go once you discover how harmful this is?

A side effect of childhood trauma is hyper-vigilance. Having been betrayed, you look for betrayal; you are watchful for anything that might hurt you; you anticipate trouble, hoping to head it off before it becomes too painful. Since your self-esteem is so low, you know that surely you must deserve something bad happening. Life becomes fearful on an almost daily basis. This hyper-vigilance becomes exhausting. Trying to escape from it leads you to addictions: alcohol, drugs, sex, and especially people addictions. The original childhood trauma, whether it is sexual abuse, physical abuse, mental or emotional abuse, continually comes out of the closet. You may not be aware of it but it is lurking in your unconscious, waiting to make an appearance as it parades back and forth prompting you to be ever watchful. Logic and reason cannot help you with this. You know something bad is about to happen and if only you can do something to control it, to ward it off, then this time it may escape you. Thus goes the mind of a human being traumatized as a child. It is hard to trust when this fear begins. You trusted before and that trust was violated. Having been betrayed once, you know it's going to happen again. And on and on it goes, this obsession and hyper-vigilance that wears you to a frazzle.

I thought I had worked hard on this during my five years of recovery. I had read the words **That which we put our attention on grows,** over and over as it sat on my "magic mirror" (a mirror upon which I had scotch taped positive sayings and then read them every day), referred to it often during my daily activities, and tried to stay disciplined about chasing away thoughts regarding things and/or people that lived in my obsession room. I found that if I didn't, they ruled my daily mental routines. The obsession room was often quite crowded. It included childhood pains, lists of men I'd slept with, and my shame at the discovery of how high those numbers were, memories of abuse suffered at the hands of males I thought I'd walked away from but who kept returning, wrongs I'd done that I continually beat myself up for, and that old standby we all use, "what if" and "if only." But thanks to recovery I knew I'd conquered all of them.

What a surprise to discover years later when I was happily married to the first healthy man in my life, that I was up to my old habits. Everything I learned, after we got married, about his history with women that appeared to be threatening found a seat in that room as it hastily became repopulated with fears. As I tried to adjust to my new marriage, I found that the information he'd shared with me about past women played out on a daily basis. It didn't help my fledgling self-confidence that his ex-girl friend lived next door and twice a day I had to pass her house.

That was always good for several minutes of fearful and obsessive mental masturbation. He had shared just enough about his relationship with her for me to have vivid mental images. I had also had several encounters with her and found her to be manipulative, controlling, and a deeply disturbing person who was bent on giving me the impression that she and my husband were still involved.

This didn't help my anxiety. No matter how often I shamed myself for not governing my thoughts (and my overactive imagination), I found that I was not in charge of the obsession room; the demons that dwelled in it were. I thought about taking a longer route home so I wouldn't have to pass her house, but decided that would mean I'd acknowledge my own weakness in being unable to control my thoughts. No matter that I knew my husband loved me and would rather take a bullet than be unfaithful; no matter that he'd been trying to avoid her for years; no matter that my logic told me that if he had loved her, he'd be with her, but he'd chosen me. After three months of marriage, she began calling obsessively. Although we usually let her messages go on the machine and Tom never returned her calls, it did little to help my growing paranoia. An ex-wife joined the badgering. Tom, a sweet and gentle person, wanted to wait it out in hopes they would both go away. After two months, it was obvious this was not going to happen. The calls became more demanding.

One time I answered the phone only to hear, "Where's Tom? And don't tell me he's at the track, I happen to know it isn't open on Sunday." Another, in a seductive manner, "Lordy, lordy, aren't you ever home anymore. How about calling me when you get home and we'll have ourselves a nice long intimate chat. I've got lots to tell you." This was from an ex-wife who had cheated on him for almost twenty years. Every couple of days, we'd come home to manipulative and suggestive phone calls.

Eventually, Tom sent an email to his ex-wife's brother telling her to go away and I put a greeting on our phone in my own seductive manner indicating, as honeymooners, we were ah...tied up. The calls stopped, but my mental obsessions did not.

The slave driver demon that was in charge of the people that inhabited that room was determined that he would jump up and scare me like the boogeyman that lived under my bed. He (and they) demanded my obsessive attention. I played over in my mind a hundred times everything I had heard about, not only the gal next door, but any other women from his past that he'd shared information with me about. Contradictions in his comments stirred up mistrust. The battle of trying to control my mind was not only wearing me out but also eroding the positive self-esteem I'd worked so hard to gain in recovery.

This wouldn't do. My husband was a patient and loving man and had learned to refuse to play in to my fears, walking out of the room and shaking his head every time I brought up yet another piece of information I'd brought up a dozen times before. I knew intellectually that they were all things we'd discussed many times before but that didn't stop me from dragging them out of my ammunition bag over and over. What had happened to that confident and wise woman he thought he'd married? He wasn't the only one who wondered. I began thinking I'd not done a good job in recovery. Had I missed something? Was I going to replay historical events forever?

I had, in my normal, "If I can only figure this out, I can make it go away" mental process (so typical of wounded children), decided that the reason I continued to obsess was because a male friend had once told me that any time a man gives a woman generalities or multiple answers to questions, he's not telling the real truth. *Aha!* There was another reason to be fearful. My husband had given me multiple answers and generalities many times as I obsessively tried to question him yet one more time. Wasn't that proof that I hadn't yet heard the final and truthful answer that would lay the matter to rest for good? Perhaps if I kept asking the same question in another manner, I'd arrive at the answer that would make me feel better. No matter that I had no idea what would make me feel better. Never mind that he was dodging accusations and mistrustful fears by thinking that if he patiently explained it this way or that, maybe I'd finally get it. I just knew there was a wrong in there somewhere and if only I could get to it, I'd be able to justify my fears.

I spent many a night tossing and turning while my husband snored innocently and obliviously away. Over and over, I played my litany of valid reasons why I was right in being fearful. Hadn't he said this one time and something different another? Hadn't he promised this and done that? Hadn't he skirted the truth with that question and so on, always looking for proof that I wasn't paranoid? The fact that I was utilizing great amounts of energy to adjust to monumental changes in my life, no longer had my support system of friends and family around me, and was further weakened with worry by potential health problems, did nothing but drain me.

I was faced with a choice. Did I want to damage our fledgling marriage or did I want to take positive steps to handle my problem? I decided I would use what was happening to write a chapter about letting go for my new book. Letting go was part of the mental and emotional dimensions of well being that I was writing about. My husband's patience was wearing thin and I was developing behavior patterns that were detrimental to the well being of our marriage. We had declared each other our best friend and here I was, treating my best friend with mistrust. It was time for drastic measures.

I thought about my recovery and how hard I had worked to get myself healthy after a lifetime of unhealthy behavior. I knew that each time I fed the mistrust, I was allowing images from relationships with former abusive spouses to surface. I was reliving the times when I had trusted and then been betrayed, parading them back and forth as if they were once again a part of my present life. Even if the images weren't at the forefront of my thoughts, they lingered like shadows behind my current fears. I thought about how for so many years I felt I was no good and the many years of work I'd done to turn that around. Did I want to throw all of it away? I took long walks and thought about what I could do to recover the ground I'd once been on. I remembered the years after recovery when my life was rich and rewarding, full of only healthy behavior patterns.

Then I took an honest assessment of my blessings. I was married to a man who was gentle and kind, who made sure that he told me he loved me several times a day; a man whom I knew to be faithful; a man with whom I had a lot in common. If we sometimes saw things in a different light—I was not interested in sacrificing integrity for niceness while he tried hard to be pleasant with others at all times—so what? If both of us had been the same, we would not have as good a chance for a successful marriage. I wanted to grow old with him; he wanted to grow old with me. We were busy doing a major remodel to make our home everything we both wanted. I loved the woods. I loved the Colorado weather, the changing of the seasons, especially the snow. We both loved good music and good books, and travel, and especially Scotland. I loved to cook and he loved my cooking. He was warm and affectionate and playful. He was the funniest man I'd ever known. He not only had accepted my large family but also loved them as if they were his own and vice versa. What was more important, I liked and respected him. I'd never been with a man I liked before, and God knows there'd been few I respected. He felt the same about me but now I needed to make sure that continued. This wasn't going to happen if I persisted in dragging up the past and obsessing on words he'd trusted me enough to share.

I started by devising my own Ten Commandments of Obsessive Behavior. Some of them were tried and true phrases

I'd heard over the years and would now need to put in practice again. They included the following:

- Thou shalt remember the number one rule: That which we put our attention on grows; that which we ignore will diminish.

- Remember that people who live in glass houses cannot afford to throw stones. Sometimes obsessing on something or someone means we are too busy judging others and not looking at our own behavior. Have we been without flaw to such a degree that we can afford to obsess on someone else's behavior?

- Remember to accent the positive and eliminate the negative.

- Thou shalt keep in mind that "hurled words, like hurled swords, can be brought back no more".

- Remember to find ways to build up your own self-esteem. A confident woman cannot be dragged down to obsessive behavior.

- Remember to look at the forest, not just the trees. One incident does not undo the good in an entire marriage. Each day is made up of actions and interactions and all of them threaded together make a whole marriage. Choose your battles wisely.

- Once a subject has been brought up, discussed and resolved, put it away. No good will come from reiterating it.

- Remember that you have choices. You can choose to assess each new situation and decide if there is truly a wrong committed, address it, and resolve it.

- Gently push away any attempts on the part of the demons in the obsession room to engage you in fear. If your intuition tells you to keep your mouth shut, listen to it. Use your head before you use your words.

- When an obsession begins to take hold and you are having a difficult time making it go away, distract yourself with a walk, a good movie, or a good book, anything pleasurable to place objectivity between your emotions and the event that set off the obsession.

I knew that I needed to cut myself some slack. Behaviors that I spent months re-creating would not go away overnight. I had to work on them on a daily basis. But the rewards in learning to let go are great. There is a difference between a perceived happening and an actual wrong. Learn to use reason to handle fears. Once you couple it with wisdom and continue to remind yourself of the Ten Commandments of Obsessive Behavior, you will be able to overcome this monumental problem. Because of working hard on my marriage, Tom and I have forged an even stronger bond than we had when first married. I still struggle with letting go. It is one of my human frailties but every time I do it, I become a better person.

21 | Creating a Vision

Now that you've learned skills in making wise decisions in the area of the six dimensions and, hopefully, are practicing them on a regular basis, it's time for the big picture. It's time to make magic happen in your life; to create a vision, and step into it. You've finally grown up and the new you can decide what you want to do with the rest of your life.

First, it is important that you differentiate between needs and wants. Even though I discussed this earlier, I'd like to elaborate here. We all have needs but not all of us have wants. We need to eat, to sleep, to remain in good health, to have others in our lives, to have a source of income etc. Wants are an entirely different matter. Most people are not even sure what their wants are. We may want an overly expensive home but can't afford it. That is certainly not a need. In fact, a strong need might be to not have that as a want. Wants are the frosting on the cake of life. Perhaps that same person, once they take care of their need— the need to get their finances in order—could make that dream home a reachable want. Most people try to take care of their wants first. They say, 'I want someone to love' when the truth is they need to deal with childhood traumas and make themselves healthy first before finding a partner for life. Otherwise, the obvious will happen. Most people can continue to live without a want. Not so with needs. You may want to have a breast implant because you are flat-chested. You may need to have a mammogram if you have a lump in that same breast.

Taking care of your needs first will free the way to have wants satisfied. Be sure you know the difference. Too many people take steps to make "wants" happen without realizing they missed the needs. My brother, Brian, wanted to drink himself into oblivion because it kept him from remembering the horror of Vietnam. He needed to get into recovery in order to have a healthy life.

A good exercise would be to make a list of your needs, then a list of your wants. Your life will become clearer then. Your list of needs may be: eating healthy, a good night's sleep, a healthy relationship with your children, a good job, etc. Your list of wants may include: a trip to England, a new house, getting your body in better shape, finding the perfect mate, writing a best-seller, etc. Have you now put your path in life in a better perspective? Believe it or not, most of your needs will be easier for they usually require no one but yourself to make them happen. Some of your wants may require the cooperation of others.

We have all seen a homeless person at the end of an off ramp carrying a sign that defines who he is. It's difficult to pass them by without feeling a pang of guilt. The only one I've ever been tempted to help is one whose sign said, "I'm a Catholic, please help me." This validates the Catholic Church's saying, "Give me a child till he's seven and he'll be mine forever". When I asked my son, who had worked undercover in the LA Police Department, what percent of homeless people use the money you give them for drugs, he replied, "100%". That is the main thing that has caused me to not hand them money. But let's use one of these homeless people as an illustration of wants vs. needs and how being unable to identify the difference between them has gotten them into their current situation. Most homeless people "want" drugs, they don't want food. They don't particularly want to work, but they need to. It's a need they are not paying attention to. I'm not saying all of them are like that. I'm sure there are some that, through unfortunate circumstances, which are no fault of their own, are now standing at the end of an off ramp. I remember a friend of mine telling me once that she stopped to make the acquaintance of one of them, told him she'd feed him if he came back to her home and do some chores for her. He was appalled at her suggestion and told her what he wanted was money. Unfortunately, he had his needs and his wants mixed up—he needed to work.

Now that you're clear about your needs and your wants, picture everything you ever wanted waiting for you. Place yourself in the midst of that vision. The new you can now make bold moves, take risks, experiment. The new you isn't afraid to ask for criticism. Get someone else's perspective on how you're doing. If you're fortunate, you'll grow and learn something new every day of your life. You are ready for change and loving it. The new you can confront any fears you have. The new you can create a positive, contagious attitude. You have become the kind of person others want to be around. You fairly hum with energy and purpose. Every day is an adventure.

Another thing that happens with the new you is that others watch how your life is changing and want to know your secret. You can lead by example, something you never thought to do. An illustration of that is my own life. Once I got into recovery and changed my unhealthy behavior, I was able to rid myself of an abusive spouse. I had two daughters who were also living with abusive spouses and in no time they too, without even getting into recovery, had gotten rid of theirs.

The list of rules I placed at the front of each chapter on the six dimensions was a suggested list. You may want to utilize it and add your own. We are all more creative than we give ourselves credit for. Sit quietly with a pencil and paper and list all events in your life and which dimension they pertain to. Then put on your optimist's hat and come up with ideas on how to improve them so that you can create your own joyful life.

Now is the time for positive imaging. I cannot tell you how many times I have either read about or heard about a highly successful person who stated that from the time they were little, they wanted to accomplish exactly what they wound up accomplishing. They saw themselves in that very position that was their heart's desire as if it were already happening. They never once lost sight of that and so made decisions and choices that kept them on the right path. Winston Churchill was invited once to make a speech during World War II while he was Prime Minister. Thousands of people gathered to hear what this great man had to say. After being introduced, he stood up, walked to the podium, cleared his throat, and said, "We will never, never, never, never give up." He then sat back down. Now there was a man with a vision. In his mind, England was going to win that war and he was able to infuse the British people with his own belief that they were invincible.

I also believe that the universe pays attention to persistence. It is as if God, or whoever my higher power is, looked over at St. Peter and said, "you know, that Marjorie McKinnon has been trying so hard to achieve her goal for so long. She has never wavered once in moving towards her dream. She deserves success, let's give it to her." I have just sold my fourth book.

Picture your own success story. Create your own vision, and then step into it.

About the Author

Marjorie McKinnon is the author of *REPAIR Your Life: A Program of Recovery from Incest & Childhood Sexual Abuse* as well as *REPAIR For Kids*. *REPAIR For Toddlers* will be published before the end of 2010. She is also the founder of The Lamplighters, a rapidly growing international movement for recovery from incest and childhood sexual abuse. The Lamplighters currently have 59 chapters in nine countries. Their  Blog is at http://www.thelamplighters.org. REPAIR is being used as a model for recovery in most of her Lamplighter chapters. One of Ms. McKinnon's goals is to initiate Lamplighter chapters in women's prisons. The California Institute for Women in Chino, CA is the home of their first prison chapter. All attendees are working the REPAIR program together.

Ms McKinnon is on the Board of Directors for the Let Go, Let Peace Come In Foundation. Their mission is to bring healing, support, and awareness to the hundreds of millions of adult childhood sexual abuse survivors and their families worldwide, and to raise money for a nonprofit fund to provide the financial assistance necessary to start survivors of childhood sexual abuse on the path to recovery "one" survivor at a time. Their website is at www.letgoletpeacecomein.org. The Foundation is currently working on establishing a World Alliance and has already partnered with NAPAC from the United Kingdom and the RAHI Foundation from India to help adult survivors recover from incest and childhood sexual abuse. They continue to identify similar Foundations with which to partner with around the globe.

Ms.McKinnon is available for speaking engagements throughout the country and in addition to her REPAIR series, is the author of five novels, three non-fiction works and five volumes of poetry.

If you would like to find the nearest Lamplighter Chapter or consider starting your own chapter, then please take a few moments to visit the Lamplighter's Blog:

http://thelamplighters.org.

Bibliography

Alcoholics Anonymous. (2007). *Alcoholics Anonymous big book: Including : personal stories for the year 2008.* S.l.: AA.

Bradshaw, J. (1988). *Healing the shame that binds you.* Deerfield Beach, Fla: Health Communications.

Bradshaw, J. (1990). *Homecoming: Reclaiming and championing your inner child.* New York: Bantam Books.

Buck, C., & Forward, S. (1989). *Toxic parents: Overcoming their hurtful legacy and reclaiming your life.* New York: Bantam Books.

Covey, S. (1999). *The 7 habits of highly effective people.* London: Simon & Schuster.

Dyer, W. W. (1976). *Your erroneous zones.* New York: Funk & Wagnalls.

Dyer, W. W. (1991). *Pulling your own strings: Dynamic techniques for dealing with other people and living your life as you choose.* New York, NY: HarperPerennial.

Farmer, S. (1989). *Adult children of abusive parents: A healing program for those who have been physically, sexually, or emotionally abused.* Los Angeles: Lowell House.

Hazelden Foundation., & Alcoholics, A. (1982). *Twenty-four hours a day.* Walker & Co.

Jeffers, S. (1997). *Feel the fear and do it anyway: How to turn your fear and indecision into confidence and action.* London: Rider.

Lieberman, L., & Westheimer, R. K. (1988). *Sex and morality: Who is teaching our sex standards?.* Boston: Harcourt Brace Jovanovich.

McKinnon, M. (2008). *Repair your life: A program of recovery from incest & childhood sexual abuse.* Ann Arbor, MI: Loving Healing Press.

McKinnon, T. W., & McKinnon, M. (2008). *Repair for kids: A children's program for recovery from incest and childhood sexual abuse.* Ann Arbor, MI: Loving Healing Press.

McWilliams, P., & McWilliams, J.-R. (2001). *You can't afford the luxury of a negative thought: A guide to positive thinking.* London: Thorsons.

Missildine, W. H. (1963). *Your inner child of the past.* New York: Simon and Schuster.

Peale, N. V. (1952). *The power of positive thinking.* New York: Prentice-Hall.

Pell, A. R., & Allen, J. (2008). *As a man thinketh & From poverty to power.* New York: J P Tarcher/Penguin.

Rothstein, L., & Borysenko, J. (1987). *Minding the body, mending the mind.* Reading, Mass: Addison-Wesley Pub. Co.

Russianoff, P. (1982). *Why do I think I am nothing without a man?.* Toronto: Bantam Books.

Smith, A. D., Rothstein, L., & Miller, L. H. (1993). *The stress solution: An action plan to manage the stress in your life.* New York: Pocket Books.

Smith, M. J. (1975). *When I say no, I feel guilty: How to cope--using the skills of systematic assertive therapy.* New York: Dial Press.

Schuller, R. H. (1983). *Tough times never last, but tough people do!.* Nashville: T. Nelson Publishers

W, B. (1957). *Alcoholics Anonymous comes of age: A brief history of A. A.* New York: Alcoholics Anonymous Pub.

Wholey, D. (1988). *Becoming your own parent: The solution for adult children of alcoholic and other dysfunctional families.* New York: Doubleday.

Index

Find Your Way to Freedom Today!

If you were abused or neglected as a child, chances are that you have been your whole life, whether you are a man, a woman, or a teen. Child abuse so mangles the personality that the victim unconsciously attracts abusers throughout the life cycle. Lies about yourself were planted deep in your mind by the abuse, and you still believe them. They are crippling your life! Do *you* have any of these signs?

- You have symptoms of Post-Traumatic Stress Disorder (PTSD).
- You feel like a second-class citizen.
- Nobody understands: they ask, "Why can't you get over it?"
- You have escaped one abuser only to end up with another.

Until you understand exactly what the abuse did to you, you cannot get free. You can stay in therapy your whole life and never get a clue. OR you can unravel the mysteries once and for all and bring everything to light by reading *AM I BAD? Recovering from Abuse*. A great resource for victims, therapists, and group work.

ISBN 978-1-932690-33-0   **List $19.95**

More information at www.RecoveringFromAbuse.com

CPSIA information can be obtained
at www.ICGtesting.com
Printed in the USA
LVOW09s0736250617

539286LV00003B/6/P